CREATING CHARACTERS USING WRITING WORKSHOP

CREATING CHARACTERS USING WRITING WORKSHOP

CHRISTINE DEPETRILLO

COMPASS
A DIVISION OF BRIGANTINE MEDIA

Creating Characters Using Writing Workshop

Published by Brigantine Media
211 North Avenue, St. Johnsbury, Vermont 05819

Cover and book design by Jacob L. Grant

Brigantine Media/Compass Publishing
211 North Avenue
St. Johnsbury, Vermont 05819
Phone: 802-751-8802
Fax: 802-751-8804
E-mail: neil@brigantinemedia.com
Website: www.brigantinemedia.com

ORDERING INFORMATION

Quantity sales
Special discounts for schools are available for quantity purchases of physical books and digital downloads. For information, contact Brigantine Media at the address shown above or visit www.brigantinemedia.com/compass.

Individual sales
Brigantine Media/Compass Publishing publications are available through most bookstores. They can also be ordered directly from Brigantine Media.
Phone: (802) 751-8802; Fax: (802) 751-8804; www.brigantinemedia.com/compass.

ISBN 978-1-9384063-3-1

CONTENTS

INTRODUCTION

It begins with a character, usually, and once he stands up on his feet and begins to move, all I can do is trot along behind him with a paper and pencil trying to keep up long enough to put down what he says and does.

WILLIAM FAULKNER

Pick up any fiction book and flip to the back cover. There is the blurb meant to grab your attention, ignite your curiosity, and empty your wallet. Those few paragraphs of text are essential for getting readers interested. How do they do it? By showing some **character**.

FROM *THE LIGHTNING THIEF* BY RICK RIORDAN

> Percy Jackson is a good kid, but he can't seem to focus on his schoolwork or control his temper. And lately, being away at boarding school is only getting worse—Percy could have sworn his pre-algebra teacher turned into a monster and tried to kill him. When Percy's mom finds out, she knows it's time that he knew the truth about where he came from, and that he go to the one place he'll be safe. She sends Percy to Camp Half Blood, a summer camp for demigods (on Long Island), where he learns that the father he never knew is Poseidon, God of the Sea. Soon a mystery unfolds and together with his friends—one a satyr and the other the demigod daughter of Athena—Percy sets out on a quest across the United States to reach the gates of the Underworld (located in a recording studio in Hollywood) and prevent a catastrophic war between the gods.

FROM *RAMONA QUIMBY, AGE 8* BY BEVERLY CLEARY

> Everything depends on Ramona.
>
> Ramona's job is to be nice to fussy Mrs. Kemp, who watches her while her mother works. If Mrs. Quimby didn't work, Mr. Quimby couldn't return to college. On top of all that, third grade isn't turning out as Ramona expected. Danny the Yard Ape teases her and, on one horrible day, she throws up—at school. Being eight isn't easy, but it's never dull!

Without characters, stories have no heartbeat, no laughter, no tears, no tension, no life. It is through characters that readers grapple with difficult problems, travel to distant lands, battle dragons, fall in love with vampires, and go on wild space adventures. Characters reach out and take readers by the hand—sometimes by the throat—and carry them along for pages and pages.

This book will help you lead your students into the world of character creation. When you use these activities with your students, they will employ the strategies authors use to develop believable and dynamic fictional characters. All the activities in this book have been used successfully with students many times. They are proven to get students excited about the writing process so they can't wait to create their own characters.

ALIGNMENT WITH COMMON CORE STATE STANDARDS

The essential skill of narrative writing is included in many of the Common Core State Standards for English Language Arts. K-12 Anchor Standard for College and Career Readiness for Writing CCRA.W.3 states that **students will be able to write narratives to develop real or imagined experiences or events**. This standard gets more specific in each grade level, requiring students to establish a situation and introduce a narrator and/or characters, as well as use dialogue and description to show the responses of characters to situations. Every activity in the book aligns with this standard as well as Anchor Standard for Language CCRA.L.3, which requires students to **apply knowledge of language to understand how language functions in different contexts.**

The activities in this book align with a number of Common Core State Standards for Reading, Writing, and Language for grades 3 through 8 as shown on the chart on pages 8 - 10.

TEACHING WITH WRITING WORKSHOP

Writing Workshop is the best format for achieving your goals for writing instruction. A well-designed, functioning Writing Workshop is a safe place for students to experiment with writing. It is nurturing, respectful, and open to the possibilities that can occur when pencil meets paper or fingers meet keyboard. Students do the work of real writers. Nothing is watered down for the classroom setting or the age group.

Writing Workshop includes the following:

Mini-lessons – These may be direct teaching on the conventions of writing (spelling, punctuation, grammar) or on the craft of writing (creating leads, developing setting, using descriptive details, creating characters).

Choice – Specific tasks are assigned to students, such as writing a fictional narrative or a certain form of poetry, but students always have choice in how they handle the task. The more open you are to their creative risk-taking, the more excited they will be to actually do the work of writing. There is no better fuel for writing than student excitement.

The Writing Process – Each writing piece students do in the Writing Workshop travels through these phases: brainstorming, planning, drafting, conferencing, revising, editing, finished product.

Conferencing – This is vital to the workshop. Professional writers get feedback from critique groups, test readers, and editors. Student writers need the same discourse. It is very hard to spot the problems in one's own work. Students can conference with a partner and should always conference with the teacher. This discussion is so important. There are many teachable moments in a one-on-one conversation about a student's writing.

Models from Published Authors – Incorporate the works of published authors to highlight certain techniques for students to try in their own writing. Emphasize to your students that these authors went through the same struggles and successes they are now going through as they write. You want students to learn not to give up, even if the writing does not come easily.

Finished Products – Any piece of writing that goes through the writing process should end up as a finished product. This is important because it highlights the importance of deadlines. Authors who don't reach the finish line don't get paid. It sets a good example for students about finishing what you start.

WRITER'S NOTEBOOK

Another mandatory piece of the Writing Workshop is the Writer's Notebook. Students *must* have one of these. It is a writer's laboratory and storage box. Students experiment with quick writing exercises in the Writer's Notebook and collect various items that may turn into writing pieces at a later date. It doesn't matter what kind of notebook is used. The student should feel comfortable with whichever notebook he/she chooses. When your students inevitably say, "I have nothing to write about," you can direct them to the treasure chest that is the Writer's Notebook. They will always find something on those pages.

WHAT TO DO WITH WRITER'S NOTEBOOKS

- collect interesting words
- record overheard conversations

- draw pictures, quick sketches, maps
- experiment with character names
- write down observations of people, animals, places, objects
- try out story titles
- write short scenes and poetry
- write memories
- make lists of things that you love, despise, fear…
- collect articles or photos that inspire you or make you wonder
- gather quotes that mean something to you
- describe regular items in detail or in unique ways
- record questions you have about anything, about everything
- write about what you notice

HOW TO USE THIS BOOK

This book is divided into four major topics that are key to creating characters:

CHAPTER 1: **Observing people** to discover elements that reveal character

CHAPTER 2: **Developing key aspects** of characters: how they look, where they live, and what they say and do

CHAPTER 3: **Character evolution** that shows how a character changes over time

CHAPTER 4: **Using voice, dialogue, and point of view** to make a character come to life

Each chapter has five activities, and each activity takes approximately 45 minutes to complete. The activities are best taught using the Writing Workshop framework, but that method of instruction is not a necessity for using the activities in this book. Most activities have graphic organizers included to guide the students. If a graphic organizer is not included, then the activity is to be completed directly in their Writer's Notebooks or on a separate sheet of paper. If you don't have the full suggested time frame for an activity, feel free to teach the lesson over more than one class period.

Students in grades three through eight can benefit from these activities, which can be reused every time a student is ready to create a new fictional character.

Each activity includes suggestions for assessment. For some activities, checklists have been created to assess student work. There are six checklists to a page, so make enough copies to have one checklist per student. Cut them apart and attach one checklist to each student's completed activity, then use the checklist for assessment. Share the contents of the checklists with each student when you conference with them about their progress. Use them to celebrate student growth and indicate areas where additional work is needed. Let them aid you in identifying where more opportunities to fine tune skills are needed. Checklists can also be shared with parents to discuss student progress in creating fictional characters.

The suggested texts in this book focus on elementary grades, but any texts containing examples of outstanding character development can be used with the lessons and graphic organizers presented here. A list of suggested texts for grades 3 through 8 is included in Appendix A (pages 99-101). Appendix B (pages102-107) includes student resources that will be helpful, and Appendix C (pages 108-109) has teacher resources with further information about teaching writing skills.

THE WRITING TEACHER MUST WRITE, TOO

A teacher of writing must also be a writer. You don't have to dream of publication or making the *New York Times* bestsellers list, but you do have to write. Every day. Your students need to see you write in your own Writer's Notebook. Make lists, jot down ideas, ask "what if" questions, sketch out scenery, play with character names, plot out different endings or deleted scenes from books or movies you love, and analyze what other authors have done correctly—writers do all of these. The more you engage in writer behavior, the more you will believe in what you are teaching your students. They, in turn, will come to respect you as an authority on writing.

If you love to write, keep writing, and use this book to help get you and your students to the next level. If writing for you is more chore than fun, do not fear. This book will make Writing Workshop and creating characters seem like the most enjoyable activities you have ever done. You won't be able to resist trying the exercises and will want nothing more than to share them with your students.

You will be a writer. So will your students. All you have to do is listen to the voices inside your head. They're characters waiting to emerge. Embrace them. Teach your students to embrace them, and by the end of this book, you'll have a host of fictional characters to include in your stories.

AS THE WRITING TEACHER, YOU SHOULD:

- Have a Writer's Notebook. Share with students why you picked that notebook and a few things you've put in it.
- Write every day. Write anything you want, but do it consistently.
- Look for ideas everywhere.
- Consider no idea ridiculous. Any idea can have a kernel of intrigue that could pop into something magnificent.
- Get excited about writing. It's an art form and should be treated with that level of whimsy and expression.
- Use the books and websites listed in the Teacher Resources section (Appendix C).
- Browse the adult and children's fiction sections of bookstores/online retailers. This helps you keep abreast of what's popular and what you and your students may want to write about.

- Read fiction. Lots of it. And notice the character development in particular. Read like a writer rather than a reader.
- Set high standards for you and your writing students. If you believe you are all writers, you are.
- Daydream.

QUESTIONS/PROMPTS FOR QUICK ASSESSMENT

Teachers need quick ways to assess student learning throughout the course of a unit, not just at the end. Use these questions/prompts while your students are working through the activities in this book to check for student understanding about the creation of fictional characters.

Post a question/prompt for all the students to see, and then have them reply on paper, which can be turned in or shared with a partner or small group. Thinking and talking about what they have learned helps students solidify the knowledge and sort through any confusion before the unit of study is over.

QUESTIONS/PROMPTS

What did you notice about characters that sticks in your head?

When I read about a character, I like to know…

I would show that a character is…(select a character trait) by…(tell how you would show that trait).

Why do characters need to change in a story?

Why do characters need a problem or obstacle?

How can you get to know a character?

What information do authors give you about characters?

How do authors give you information about characters?

What makes a character believable?

ASSESSMENT AND FEEDBACK

Some of the activities in the book include checklists that may be used for assessment purposes. You may have your own district-approved assessment rubrics that you use. Another source of rubrics for grading student writing is Ruth Culham's *6 + 1 Traits of Writing*.

Meaningful feedback from you is the most valuable assessment a writing student can receive. Positive, constructive feedback helps students recognize their strengths and gain confidence in their developing abilities. Your feedback will also help them locate areas of need and give them steps to make improvements.

A writer once said that there is no such thing as a "final draft." There are always revisions that can be made to enhance the piece. When assessing student writing, it is important to give opportunities for students to use the comments and suggestions you've made. They need chances to take another look...and another...and another, until they've achieved the standards addressed and have created something they are proud to call their own. When you allow time for revision, you will be helping to develop writers who think reflectively about their work and aren't afraid to cross things out and take another stab at it. This is a vital lesson for any writer to learn.

One of my readers told me that a fictional character I created was exactly like her grandfather. I had never met her grandfather, of course, but the character was so three-dimensional, he reminded the reader of a real person. That's what you want to help your students achieve. Using the activities in this book, your students will learn to create characters that seem so real, they breathe!

A NOTE ABOUT WRITERS

The best way to learn to write is to...write. You don't get to be a marathon runner by reading about running or watching others run. Runners run. Painters paint. Woodworkers woodwork.

Writers write.

I've been writing since I discovered how well red crayon showed up on the white walls of my childhood bedroom. My parents could have screamed at me, but they didn't. Instead, they introduced me to paper, and I haven't stopped loving both the work and joy of writing.

For students, writing can be a daunting task. They may not have any ideas. Maybe they can't spell or don't know interesting words to use. Perhaps punctuation and grammar are like those annoying older cousins that tease them at family gatherings. Some students may think they are not writers.

They'd be wrong.

We are *all* writers.

As humans, the desire to communicate is innate. From our earliest moments, we are driven to make our needs known. We eventually learn the words that make conveying these needs to others easier. Soon we wish to share more than just our needs. We have thoughts and wants and ideas and emotions. Developing fictional characters is no different. Characters have needs, thoughts, wants, ideas, and emotions just like the rest of us, whether they are human, animal, or something dark and creepy. These characters are inside all of us.

We may not know it, and that's where writing teachers—you—play a vital role. You are the Key Master, ready to help students unlock their writing potential. You may also have to be the Lighthouse Keeper, because many students will not see their abilities. They will only see the stormy, disorienting sea of a blank page. It's up to you to shine a light on what your students can accomplish.

It's exciting to work with budding Patricia Polaccos, Roald Dahls, Gary Paulsens, Sharon Creeches, J.R.R. Tolkiens, and J.D. Salingers who may be sitting in your classroom. These students are waiting for you to light their creative candles and help them bring life to the characters hiding inside them.

WRITING

ALIGNS WITH ACTIVITIES	COMMON CORE STATE STANDARDS BY GRADE LEVEL
WRITING **All Activities**	**W.3.3a** Establish a situation and introduce a narrator and/or characters; organize an event sequence that unfolds naturally. **W.3.3b** Use dialogue and descriptions of actions, thoughts, and feelings to develop experiences and events or show the response of characters to situations. **W.4.3a** Orient the reader by establishing a situation and introducing a narrator and/or characters; organize an event sequence that unfolds naturally. **W.4.3b** Use dialogue and description to develop experiences and events or show the responses of characters to situations. **W.5.3a** Orient the reader by establishing a situation and introducing a narrator and/or characters; organize an event sequence that unfolds naturally. **W.5.3b** Use narrative techniques, such as dialogue, description, and pacing, to develop experiences and events or show the responses of characters to situations. **W.6.3a** Engage and orient the reader by establishing a context and introducing a narrator and/or characters; organize an event sequence that unfolds naturally and logically. **W.6.3b** Use narrative techniques, such as dialogue, pacing, and description, to develop experiences, events, and/or characters. **W.7.3a** Engage and orient the reader by establishing a context and point of view and introducing a narrator and/or characters; organize an event sequence that unfolds naturally and logically. **W.7.3b** Use narrative techniques, such as dialogue, pacing, and description, to develop experiences, events, and/or characters. **W.8.3a** Engage and orient the reader by establishing a context and point of view and introducing a narrator and/or characters; organize an event sequence that unfolds naturally and logically. **W.8.3b** Use narrative techniques, such as dialogue, pacing, description, and reflection, to develop experiences, events, and/or characters.

ALIGNS WITH ACTIVITIES	COMMON CORE STATE STANDARDS BY GRADE LEVEL
LANGUAGE All Activities	**L.3.3** Use knowledge of language and its conventions when writing, speaking, reading, or listening.
	L.3.3a Choose words and phrases for effect.
	L.4.3 Use knowledge of language and its conventions when writing, speaking, reading, or listening.
	L.4.3a Choose words and phrases to convey ideas precisely.
	L.4.3b Choose punctuation for effect.
	L.5.3 Use knowledge of language and its conventions when writing, speaking, reading, or listening.
	L.6.3 Use knowledge of language and its conventions when writing, speaking, reading, or listening.
	L.6.3b Maintain consistency in style and tone.
	L.7.3 Use knowledge of language and its conventions when writing, speaking, reading, or listening.
	L.8.3 Use knowledge of language and its conventions when writing, speaking, reading, or listening.
Activities: 1.1, 1.3, 4.1, 4.2	**L.3.5** Demonstrate understanding of figurative language, word relationships and nuances in word meanings.
	L.4.5 Demonstrate understanding of figurative language, word relationships, and nuances in word meanings.
	L.5.5 Demonstrate understanding of figurative language, word relationships, and nuances in word meanings.
	L.6.5 Demonstrate understanding of figurative language, word relationships, and nuances in word meanings.
	L.7.5 Demonstrate understanding of figurative language, word relationships, and nuances in word meanings.
	L.8.5 Demonstrate understanding of figurative language, word relationships, and nuances in word meanings.

READING

ALIGNS WITH ACTIVITIES	COMMON CORE STATE STANDARDS BY GRADE LEVEL
READING LITERATURE **Activities 1.3, 1.4, 2.1, 3.1, 3.2, 3.4, 4.3**	**RL.3.3** Describe characters in a story (e.g., their traits, motivations, or feelings) and explain how their actions contribute to the sequence of events. **RL.4.3** Describe in depth a character, setting, or event in a story or drama, drawing on specific details in the text (e.g., a character's thoughts, words, or actions). **RL.5.3** Compare and contrast two or more characters, settings, or events in a story or drama, drawing on specific details in the text (e.g., how characters interact). **RL.6.3** Describe how a particular story's or drama's plot unfolds in a series of episodes as well as how the characters respond or change as the plot moves toward a resolution. **RL.7.3** Analyze how particular elements of a story or drama interact (e.g., how setting shapes the characters or plot). **RL.8.3** Analyze how particular lines of dialogue or incidents in a story or drama propel the action, reveal aspects of a character, or provoke a decision.
Activities 4.4, 4.5	**RL.3.6** Distinguish their own point of view from that of the narrator or those of the characters. **RL.4.6** Compare and contrast the point of view from which different stories are narrated, including the difference between first- and third-person narrations. **RL.5.6** Describe how a narrator's or speaker's point of view influences how events are described. **RL.6.6** Explain how an author develops the point of view of the narrator or speaker in a text. **RL.7.6** Analyze how an author develops and contrasts the points of view of different characters or narrators in a text. **RL.8.6** Analyze how differences in the points of view of the characters and the audience or reader (e.g., created through the use of dramatic irony) create such effects as suspense or humor.

OBSERVING
Characters

Ideas for characters are all around us. The sassy gal at the convenience store register. The solemn man sitting on the bus reading a how-to book about composting. The playful puppy romping around your neighbor's yard. Just by watching them, we can find elements useful for developing believable characters.

Observation is a writer's most valuable tool. Talk to your students about how to observe people when beginning to create characters:

- Pay attention to how people walk. Do they have long strides? What sound do their shoes make? Do they swing their arms when they walk?
- Notice how people's faces change when they are talking with someone else. Do their brows crinkle together? Do they chew on their bottom lip? Do they look at the speaker or around at other things?
- Zoom in on how people dress. Do they tuck their shirts in? Are their pants freshly pressed? Do they zip their coats or let them flap open?

Picking up on the subtleties of people's behavior helps a writer add these quirks to fictional characters to make them more real. Writers notice everything around them. They pick up on the details that other people ignore. Encourage students to record such details in their Writer's Notebooks for future use.

IN THIS CHAPTER:

Five activities are included to help your students use observation as a writing tool to start creating characters.

ACTIVITY 1.1: Observe character traits of real people.

ACTIVITY 1.2: Create a character with those observed traits, writing about the character in a fictional situation.

ACTIVITIES 1.3 AND 1.4: Study published authors' characters and the students' favorite characters to identify what works in fiction. Learn how authors show character traits through a character's words, thoughts, feelings, and actions.

ACTIVITY 1.5: Start creating their own fictional characters.

Activity #1.1

LOOKING CLOSELY

Observing a real person's details can help create believable characters.

NEED

- Volunteers to be observed
- **Looking Closely** graphic organizers, Forms A or B (one per student)
- Slips of 2-inch by 11-inch paper (one per student)

TIME: 50 MINUTES

- 30 minutes for observation
- 20 minutes for follow-up sharing and discussion

COMMON CORE ANCHOR STANDARDS

WRITING:

W.3 Write narratives to develop real or imagined experiences or events using effective technique, well-chosen details and well-structured event sequences.

LANGUAGE:

L.3 Apply knowledge of language to understand how language functions in different contexts, to make effective choices for meaning or style, and to comprehend more fully when reading or listening.

L.5 Demonstrate understanding of figurative language, word relationships, and nuances in word meanings.

WHAT TO DO

1 Have students pick a person to study for at least thirty minutes. You can assign this as a homework assignment or do it during class time, enlisting the help of your school colleagues who don't mind being watched.

2 Students observe this person *without talking to him or her* and record everything they notice on the **Looking Closely** graphic organizer (use version A for a more open-ended response or version B for a more structured response, depending on your students' needs). This works best if the person being observed is in the middle of an activity such as baking, conversing with another person, teaching, managing students in the cafeteria, or building something. The more action the person is performing, the more your students will witness. Tell students to focus on the details and notice as much as they can. Even the simplest observation can be important.

3 When students return to class with their completed graphic organizers, have them partner up and share three things they noticed about the person they observed. For example, a student may say that his father puts on his left shoe before his

right one. Someone else may share that the school principal listens to country music when she's working in her office. Another student may reveal that her soccer coach keeps two extra hair elastics on her wrist during practice. By sharing observations, students may get additional ideas for traits to give their own fictional characters.

Borrowing the habits and mannerisms of real people is a perfectly fine way to build a fictional character.

4 Have each student write on a large slip of paper one thing they observed. Post all the observations in the classroom where everyone can see them.

5 Have a five-minute class discussion on what students find most interesting about the information collected. Emphasize that each of the posted items shows us something about the person, and that these little quirks are what make the observed people real and unique. Let students know that when they are developing their own characters, observations like the posted ones can be used. They don't have to invent everything from scratch. Borrowing the habits and mannerisms of real people is a perfectly fine way to build a fictional character.

ASSESSMENT

Informal assessing can occur during the sharing and discussion portions of the exercise.

Name: ______________________ Date: __________

Looking Closely – A

DIRECTIONS

Choose one person to observe closely for thirty minutes. Do not talk to this person. Just watch what the person does in the thirty-minute time period and record what you see. Try to be as detailed as you can.

Name of person observed: ______________________

Activity he/she is doing: ______________________

Location during observation: ______________________

OBSERVATION NOTES

Name: ______________________ Date: __________

Looking Closely – A

DIRECTIONS

Choose one person to observe closely for thirty minutes. Do not talk to this person. Just watch what the person does in the thirty-minute time period and record what you see. Try to be as detailed as you can.

Name of person observed: Sal

Activity he/she is doing: Landscaping

Location during observation: Neighbor's front yard

OBSERVATION NOTES

-wearing shorts, tan work boots, green T-shirt with "Sal's Landscaping" on the back, work gloves, Red Sox baseball cap

-two different colored socks, one green, one white, jingly key ring on his belt

-mows the lawn with a riding mower, trims the branches of a Japanese maple tree with huge clippers, weeds the garden around the pond, carries huge rocks to border the pond

-listens to iPod, sometimes sings out loud, voice is kind of scratchy, but good

-drinks from a huge water bottle

-talks to Rob, owner of the house, about fixing his front walkway that is crumbling, takes baseball cap off when he talks to Rob and hangs iPod earphones around his neck

-smiles a lot, laughs with Rob, drinks lemonade from Cindy, Rob's daughter

-pets Rob's dog, Cesar, until the dog runs off with a work glove

Name: ______________________________ Date: ______________

Looking Closely – B

DIRECTIONS

Choose one person to observe closely for thirty minutes. Do not talk to this person. Just watch what the person does in the thirty-minute time period and record what you see. Try to be as detailed as you can.

Who did you observe?______________________________

____

What did this person do?______________________________

____

What did this person say?______________________________

____

What did this person use to do his/her activity?______________________________

____

What did you hear when you observed this person?______________________________

____

Describe the place where you observed this person. ______________________________

____

What kind of mood was this person in today?______________________________

____

Did this person interact with any other people while you observed? If so, with whom? What happened during the interaction?______________________________

____

____

____

What else did you notice during the observation?______________________________

____

____

____

____

Name: ____________________ Date: __________

Looking Closely – B

DIRECTIONS

Choose one person to observe closely for thirty minutes. Do not talk to this person. Just watch what the person does in the thirty-minute time period and record what you see. Try to be as detailed as you can.

Who did you observe? Sal

What did this person do? mowed the lawn, trimmed tree branches, weeded the garden, carried rocks

What did this person say? talked to Rob about fixing the front walk

What did this person use to do his/her activity? riding mower, huge clippers

What did you hear when you observed this person? I heard Sal singing along to his iPod

Describe the place where you observed this person. my neighbor Rob's front yard

What kind of mood was this person in today? Sal seemed to be in a happy mood. He smiled a lot, sang to himself, and laughed with Rob.

Did this person interact with any other people while you observed? If so, with whom? What happened during the interaction? He drank lemonade that Cindy, Rob's daughter, brought him.

What else did you notice during the observation? He hangs his iPod earphones around his neck. He wore two different colored socks, one green, one white. He has a jingly key ring on his belt. Sal petted Rob's dog, Cesar, until the dog ran off with a work glove. He drank from a huge water bottle.

Activity #1.2

WHAT WOULD THEY DO?

Convey character traits to readers through a character's response to a situation.

NEED

- Completed **Looking Closely** graphic organizers (from Activity 1.1)
- **Character Traits** sheet (one per student), page 20
- Writer's Notebooks

TIME: 50 MINUTES

- 30 minutes for observation
- 20 minutes for follow-up sharing and discussion

COMMON CORE ANCHOR STANDARDS

WRITING:

W.3 Write narratives to develop real or imagined experiences or events using effective technique, well-chosen details and well-structured event sequences.

LANGUAGE:

L.3 Apply knowledge of language to understand how language functions in different contexts, to make effective choices for meaning or style, and to comprehend more fully when reading or listening.

WHAT TO DO

1 Have students review their observation notes from the **Looking Closely** activity. Using the **Character Traits** list (page 20) or their own words, students should assign three character traits to the person they observed. For example, they may say that the school secretary is *efficient*, *cheerful*, and *organized*.

2 Present Situations A, B, and C. Instruct students to choose one situation and write a short scene in their own Writer's Notebooks in which they show how their observed person would react to the situation they've selected.

SITUATION A	SITUATION B	SITUATION C
A mysterious package is found on your person's doorstep. What does he/she do?	Someone throws a surprise birthday party for your person. What is his/her reaction?	Your person is on a sinking sailboat. What does he/she do?

These three situations should work for most students, but feel free to create other situations that may be a better fit for your class or the types of people your students have observed. Give students about 20 minutes to write.

QUESTIONS TO ASK STUDENTS

What evidence do you have that makes you think your person would react that way?

What would your person say, think, feel, and do in this situation?

What character traits are you showing?

Can you tell me more about…? (insert whatever you may want them to further explore)

3 Have students share their scenes with a partner. Move around the room and check with each pair to get a feel for how well students have incorporated what they have observed into their scenes.

4 Select a few students who have done a good job to share their scenes with the class. Point out what works in their pieces, or ask other students what works. Highlight the believability of their people's reactions and the descriptive details that show their character traits.

5 Activities 1.1 and 1.2 can be repeated as many times as you think it necessary to help students learn that ideas for characters can be found in the people around us.

ASSESSMENT

Informal assessing can happen during the sharing, checking in with students, and discussion portions of the exercise.

CHARACTER TRAITS

Outgoing	Emotional	Charming	Kind	Brave
Gloomy	Intelligent	Funny	Afraid	Strong
Weak	Nervous	Confident	Quiet	Loud
Friendly	Clever	Boring	Thoughtful	Angry
Happy	Solemn	Guilty	Worried	Independent
Determined	Adventurous	Honest	Chatty	Secretive
Forgiving	Unforgiving	Opinionated	Unique	Patient
Impatient	Suspicious	Hopeful	Hopeless	Efficient
Cheerful	Trusting	Insecure	Popular	Gullible
Quirky	Impulsive	Controlling	Flexible	Inflexible
Lonely	Challenging	Devious	Shy	Laid back
Sarcastic	Silly	Compassionate	Fair	Honorable
Loyal	Responsible	Trustworthy	Bitter	Demanding
Greedy	Jealous	Unreliable	Reliable	Serious
Reckless	Curious	Dishonest	Bubbly	Grouchy
Clumsy	Cowardly	Wise	Picky	Plain
Leader	Expert	Mischievous	Fancy	Messy
Excited	Inventive	Creative	Gentle	Pretty
Neat	Poor	Rich	Ugly	Stubborn

WHAT WOULD THEY DO?

Sample Entry in Writer's Notebook

Character traits: Sal is humorous, curious, and strong.

Situation A

Sal came home after a long day of landscaping. Everyone's yard in the neighborhood looked fantastic...except his. Weeds grew taller than the porch railings. Leaves were scattered all around the lawn, which was in need of a cut. The flowers in the window boxes drooped from the beating sun of a hot, summer day.

"I'm too tired to landscape my own yard," Sal said aloud.

A bluejay cawed in the old oak tree, the one whose branches scraped against Sal's bedroom window whenever there was a breeze. The bird seemed to be saying, Get to work, Sal.

"Aww, be quiet." Sal pointed at the nagging bluejay then climbed the peeling steps of his porch. A huge package wrapped in brown paper waited at his front door. It was long and rectangular.

"What's this?" He tossed a glance around his yard, but the only one around was that bluejay, still cawing and nagging, nagging and cawing.

Fishing his key out of his pocket, he lifted the package with a groan and went inside. He dropped the large package onto his kitchen table and studied it from all sides.

"No company name on the outside," he said. "No return address." He glanced to the calendar hanging by the refrigerator. "Not my birthday. Not Christmas..."

He tore off the paper on the package to find...

Activity #1.3

STUDYING THE EXPERTS

Examine how authors develop a character.

NEED

- **Studying the Experts** graphic organizers (one per student)
- **Character Traits** sheet (one per student), page 20
- Appropriate level books/excerpts with well-developed characters

TIME: 45 MINUTES

- 30 minutes to study characters
- 15 minutes for follow up sharing and discussion

COMMON CORE ANCHOR STANDARDS

WRITING:

W.3 Write narratives to develop real or imagined experiences or events using effective technique, well-chosen details and well-structured event sequences.

LANGUAGE:

L.3 Apply knowledge of language to understand how language functions in different contexts, to make effective choices for meaning or style, and to comprehend more fully when reading or listening.

L.5 Demonstrate understanding of figurative language, word relationships, and nuances in word meanings.

READING:

RL.3 Describe in depth a character, setting, or event in a story or drama, drawing on specific details in the text (e.g., a character's thoughts, words, or actions).

WHAT TO DO

1. Have students select three characters from books they have read. It would be best to have the texts or excerpts available for this activity so students can refer to them.
2. Have students fill out the **Studying the Experts** graphic organizer to identify the character, determine character traits, and supply evidence of the author showing those character traits. Students can work in teams on this exercise, and you should encourage discussion among partners. Students who are actively discussing the characters they are studying learn to think on a deeper level.

3 Move around the room to each team to help students see how authors reveal information through what characters say, think, feel, and do. Other characters often reveal things about the protagonist or antagonist. Help students notice that authors *show*, not tell. For example, instead of saying, "Sally was a friendly girl," an author will show Sally welcoming a new student to her class. Readers then infer that Sally is friendly.

4 Hold a whole class discussion after students have completed their **Studying the Experts** graphic organizers. Have some students share their discoveries and take every opportunity to emphasize what the published authors have done well to develop characters.

Authors *show*, not tell, about characters. Personality and character traits are best demonstrated through action.

ASSESSMENT

Informal assessing can occur during the conferences with students and the whole class discussion. The completed **Studying the Experts** graphic organizer can be used as a formal assessment.

Name: ____________________ Date: __________

Studying the Experts

DIRECTIONS

Choose three characters from books you have read and list two character traits for each. Supply evidence from the text to show how the author lets readers know about each of those character traits.

CHARACTER'S NAME/TITLE OF BOOK	CHARACTER TRAITS	TEXT EVIDENCE

Name: ________________ Date: ________

Studying the Experts

DIRECTIONS

Choose three characters from books you have read and list two character traits for each. Supply evidence from the text to show how the author lets readers know about each of those character traits.

CHARACTER'S NAME/BOOK TITLE	CHARACTER TRAITS	TEXT EVIDENCE
Evan Treski/The Lemonade War	Conflicted	"He was starting to feel words piling up inside him, crowding his lungs, forcing out all the air."
	Insecure	"His math papers from school were always covered in X's. Nobody else got as many X's as he did."
Aubrey/Love, Aubrey	independent	"I had everything I needed to run a household: a house, food, and a new family. From now on it would just be me, Aubrey, and Sammy—the two of us, and no one else."
	scared	"No more answering the phone; it was too risky." "I couldn't let anyone, anyone, know that I was alone."

Activity #1.4

YOUR FAVORITE CHARACTER

Focus on what makes a favorite character memorable.

NEED

- Writer's Notebooks

TIME: 30 MINUTES

- 15 minutes to write
- 15 minutes for follow up sharing and discussion

COMMON CORE ANCHOR STANDARDS

WRITING:

W.3 Write narratives to develop real or imagined experiences or events using effective technique, well-chosen details and well-structured event sequences.

LANGUAGE:

L.3 Apply knowledge of language to understand how language functions in different contexts, to make effective choices for meaning or style, and to comprehend more fully when reading or listening.

READING:

RL.3 Describe in depth a character, setting, or event in a story or drama, drawing on specific details in the text (e.g., a character's thoughts, words, or actions).

WHAT TO DO

1. In their Writer's Notebooks, have students select their favorite character from a book, television show, or movie. It can be something they've read or seen recently or an old favorite.
2. Tell them to describe that character as if they were telling someone who had never heard of the character before. They should also include why they like that character. Give them about fifteen minutes to write.

QUESTIONS TO ASK TO HELP STUDENTS

Why does that character stick in your mind?

What makes that character memorable?

Can you identify with this character? How?

When the time is up, ask some students to share with the whole group.

ASSESSMENT

Informal assessment can rise out of the discussion of characters.

YOUR FAVORITE CHARACTER

Sample Entry in Writer's Notebook

My Favorite Character

My favorite character is Scooby-Doo. He is a huge, tannish dog who likes to solve mysteries with Shaggy and the gang. He has a funny laugh and a sloppy lick. I like Scooby-Doo because he reminds me of my dog, Rudy. They are both very curious and sometimes get into trouble because of that. Both dogs also love snacks. Scooby-Doo sticks in my mind because he thinks how a real dog probably thinks. He's also loyal and caring, especially when it comes to Shaggy. I'd like to own Scooby-Doo. I think we would have lots of fun together.

Activity #1.5

GOALS, MOTIVATION, AND CONFLICT

Begin to develop your own fictional character with goals, motivation, and conflict. Is the character a human, an animal, or something else?

NEED

- **Goals, Motivation, and Conflict** graphic organizer (one per student)
- **Checklists for Goals, Motivation, and Conflict** (one per student)

TIME: 45 MINUTES

- 30 minutes to complete graphic organizer
- 15 minutes follow-up sharing and discussion

SUGGESTED TEXT

The City of Ember by Jeanne DuPrau, or other books with back cover text that highlights the characters' goals, motivation, and conflict

COMMON CORE ANCHOR STANDARDS

WRITING:

W.3 Write narratives to develop real or imagined experiences or events using effective technique, well-chosen details and well-structured event sequences.

LANGUAGE:

L.3 Apply knowledge of language to understand how language functions in different contexts, to make effective choices for meaning or style, and to comprehend more fully when reading or listening.

WHAT TO DO

1. Students complete the **Goals, Motivation, and Conflict** graphic organizer. This activity is intended to help students figure out what their characters hope to achieve over the course of their story, why their characters want what they want, and what is going to try to stand in their way of reaching their goals.
2. As students fill in the **Goals, Motivation, and Conflict** graphic organizers, conference briefly with them.

QUESTIONS TO ASK STUDENTS

What does your character want that he/she/it does not have now?

Why does your character want that?

Is that a believable goal for your character? Why?

Who could make things difficult for your character?

Why would so-and-so stand in your character's way?

What kinds of conflicts could a character like yours have?

Other questions will arise as you deal with the specific characters your students wish to create. If any students are struggling with this activity, direct them to read the back covers of several books in the classroom library. Guide them through identifying what the main character in those books wants and what is standing in his/her/its way. For example, the back cover of *The City of Ember* by Jeanne DuPrau reads:

> Lina Mayfleet desperately wants to be a messenger. Instead, she draws the dreaded job of Pipeworks laborer, which means she'll be working in damp tunnels deep underground.
>
> Doon Harrow draws messenger—and asks Lina to trade! Doon *wants* to be underground. That's where the generator is, and Doon has ideas about how to fix it. For as long as anyone can remember, the great lights of Ember have kept the endless darkness at bay. But now the lights are beginning to flicker...

This is a good book to use to help students, because the back cover text clearly states what each character wants, what is in the character's way, and the story's main conflict.

ASSESSMENT

Use the **Checklists for Goals, Motivation, and Conflict** to assess students on this activity.

Name: ______________________ Date: ____________

Goals, Motivation, and Conflict

DIRECTIONS

Help to define your character's goal, motivation, and conflict by filling in the blanks.

My character's name is ______________________

My character is a/an ______________________
(give age and species; for example, a one-year old unicorn, or a ten-year old boy)

My character wants *(for example, to fly, or to find his dad, or to overcome her fear of spiders)*

____

____

My character wants this because ______________________

____

____

______________________ **will get in the way of my character getting what he/she/it wants.** *(Tell who or what will make things difficult for your character.)*

Name: ____________________ Date: __________

Goals, Motivation, and Conflict

DIRECTIONS

Help to define your character's goal, motivation, and conflict by filling in the blanks.

My character's name is Zeffer Hampton.

My character is a/an twelve-year old boy.
(give age and species; for example, a one-year old unicorn, or a ten-year old boy)

My character wants *(for example, to fly, or to find his dad, or to overcome her fear of spiders)*
to get back home to Earth after being picked up by aliens.

My character wants this because he misses his normal life.

The aliens thinking he can save them from their enemies **will get in the way of my character getting what he/she/it wants.** *(Tell who or what will make things difficult for your character.)*

Goals, Motivation, and Conflict Development

GOALS, MOTIVATION, AND CONFLICT DEVELOPMENT	GOALS, MOTIVATION, AND CONFLICT DEVELOPMENT
Student Name: ________ Date: ________ ☐ Character has a clear, believable goal. ☐ Character has realistic motivation for wanting to reach that goal. ☐ A reasonable conflict has been determined. Comments: ________	Student Name: ________ Date: ________ ☐ Character has a clear, believable goal. ☐ Character has realistic motivation for wanting to reach that goal. ☐ A reasonable conflict has been determined. Comments: ________
GOALS, MOTIVATION, AND CONFLICT DEVELOPMENT	**GOALS, MOTIVATION, AND CONFLICT DEVELOPMENT**
Student Name: ________ Date: ________ ☐ Character has a clear, believable goal. ☐ Character has realistic motivation for wanting to reach that goal. ☐ A reasonable conflict has been determined. Comments: ________	Student Name: ________ Date: ________ ☐ Character has a clear, believable goal. ☐ Character has realistic motivation for wanting to reach that goal. ☐ A reasonable conflict has been determined. Comments: ________
GOALS, MOTIVATION, AND CONFLICT DEVELOPMENT	**GOALS, MOTIVATION, AND CONFLICT DEVELOPMENT**
Student Name: ________ Date: ________ ☐ Character has a clear, believable goal. ☐ Character has realistic motivation for wanting to reach that goal. ☐ A reasonable conflict has been determined. Comments: ________	Student Name: ________ Date: ________ ☐ Character has a clear, believable goal. ☐ Character has realistic motivation for wanting to reach that goal. ☐ A reasonable conflict has been determined. Comments: ________

GETTING TO KNOW *Characters* 2

How do you get to know the people you meet? You ask questions.

How long have you lived in town? What do you do for work? Do you have any children? What was your childhood like? What's your favorite food, type of music, vacation spot? Are you a cat person, a dog person, or both? Do you prefer summer or winter? It's fun asking questions like these when you are first getting to know someone. Developing characters is no different than asking these questions.

An idea for a character may present itself in various ways. I sometimes hear a rogue voice in my head saying something I wouldn't normally think of myself. This voice is a character trying to free himself or herself or, on occasion, itself. The only way to understand this character is to ask questions.

Other times, I get character ideas from hearing about interesting jobs. If I read enough about the occupation, it isn't long before the face of a person who does the job appears in my mind or lines of dialogue sound in my ear. Then I have to ask questions to get all the necessary details.

Most elementary students aren't tuned in to jobs, but they can look for character ideas in the hobbies or sports they enjoy. Reading about what they like to do can get children daydreaming about other people who like those activities, and daydreaming is a very good habit to encourage for writers of any age.

In order to write their stories effectively, students need to know their characters very well. Actually, a character who has been properly developed writes his or her *own* story with little effort needed on the part of the author. Encourage students to let their characters lead the way.

Students should spend time with their characters.

Well-crafted characters take on lives of their own. They make decisions. They make mistakes. They make discoveries. The only way to figure out how characters do these things is to talk to them as if they were real. Yes, it may look like you're asking students to talk to themselves, but every character one creates is a little piece of oneself, even if the character is a magical unicorn or a fire-eating troll.

Students should spend time with their characters. Some characters are shy. They need a little time to coalesce. Your students need time to understand their characters before they can write them into a believable story.

Now that your students are beginning to think about their characters, they need to get to know them well. The five activities in this chapter will help them discover who their characters really are, so they will be ready to create them for others to meet on the page.

IN THIS CHAPTER:

ACTIVITY 2.1: "Interview" a character from a book.

ACTIVITY 2.2: Draw and describe their characters' physical appearance.

ACTIVITY 2.3: "Interview" the fictional character they are creating.

ACTIVITY 2.4: Draw and describe the fictional character's main setting.

ACTIVITY 2.5: Describe one item that is very important to the character they are creating.

Activity #2.1

INTERVIEW A BOOK CHARACTER

"Interview" a book's character, using the character descriptions to infer how that character would respond to the interview questions.

NEED

- **Interview a Book Character** graphic organizers (one per student)
- **Character Traits** sheet (page 20)
- Appropriate level books/excerpts with well-developed characters

TIME: 45 MINUTES

- 30 minutes to interview characters
- 15 minutes follow-up sharing and discussion

SUGGESTED TEXT

See "Suggested Texts" chart (pages 99-100)

COMMON CORE ANCHOR STANDARDS

WRITING:

W.3 Write narratives to develop real or imagined experiences or events using effective technique, well-chosen details and well-structured event sequences.

LANGUAGE:

L.3 Apply knowledge of language to understand how language functions in different contexts, to make effective choices for meaning or style, and to comprehend more fully when reading or listening.

READING:

RL.3 Describe in depth a character, setting, or event in a story or drama, drawing on specific details in the text (e.g., a character's thoughts, words, or actions).

WHAT TO DO

1. Pair up students and instruct them to choose a book character they know well. If students have trouble selecting or agreeing upon a character, provide them with a list of characters in books they have already read.
2. Students conduct a mock interview with the chosen character, using the **Interview a Book Character** graphic organizer. One student takes the role of the reporter doing the asking and recording of answers. The other student acts as the character, answering the questions as the character would.
3. Halfway through the activity, stop students and have them swap roles. The reporter finishes as the character answering the questions, and the character takes on the reporter role to ask the remaining questions.

4. When students complete the interview, they should team up with another pair and share their interviews.
5. Bring the whole class back together and ask some students to share one thing that surprised them during their interviews.

ASSESSMENT

Informal assessment can occur during the sharing and discussion portions of the activity. The graphic organizer can be collected and evaluated as well.

Name: ______________________ Date: ____________

Interview a Book Character

DIRECTIONS

Choose a book character. One partner is the reporter asking the following questions and recording responses. The other partner is the character answering the questions. Try to answer as the character would and be as detailed as you can. Add any other questions you may think will work.

What is your name?

____

What is your family like?

____

____

How would you describe yourself?

____

____

____

Where do you live?

____

____

What is your idea of a "perfect day?"

____

____

____

____

What is the worst thing that has happened to you?

____

____

What do you look for in a friend?

____

____

Name: ______________________________ Date: ______________

Interview a Book Character — Page 2

What are you afraid of?

____

____

What plans do you have for yourself?

____

What do you like to do?

____

____

Where would you like to visit?

____

What is your favorite____________?______________________________
(pick something such as color, food, animal)

Name: ______________________ Date: __________

Interview A Book Character

DIRECTIONS

Choose a book character. One partner is the reporter asking the following questions and recording responses. The other partner is the character answering the questions. Try to answer as the character would and be as detailed as you can. Add any other questions you may think will work.

What is your name?

Jessie Treski (from The Lemonade War)

What is your family like?

My family includes my mom and my brother, Evan, who is usually my best friend, but ever since that letter came, he seems to be mad at me.

How would you describe yourself?

I am a person who loves numbers. I can listen to a problem with numbers and solve it in my head. I'm not so good at deciding if people are being nice to me or making fun of me. That's where Evan usually helps me, but not now. Now, he is still mad.

Where do you live?

I live in Massachusetts in a neighborhood of thirsty neighbors who want to buy my lemonade.

What is your idea of a "perfect day?"

My idea of a perfect day would be one where Evan and I have our lemonade stand and people are lined up around the block to buy. We make a ton of money that I will save in my box, but Evan will spend on a new iPod, which is fine because he'll let me pick out a few songs...you know, when he's not mad at me.

What is the worst thing that has happened to you?

My dad leaving was terrible. Evan being mad at me when I don't even know why is pretty yucky too.

What do you look for in a friend?

I look for someone who likes numbers like me. Someone who wants to play games and make stuff. Someone who won't get mad at me when I didn't even do anything.

Name: ______________________ Date: __________

Interview a Book Character — Page 2

What are you afraid of?

I'm nervous about skipping third grade and starting fourth grade, Evan's grade. But it should be okay because I'll be in Evan's class just like the letter said.

What plans do you have for yourself?

I plan to have my own business where I can work with numbers all day.

What do you like to do?

I like to ride my bike, have lemonade stands, read, write, swim, play with Evan (when he's talking to me).

Where would you like to visit?

I'd like to visit just about anywhere. I haven't really been too far away from home yet.

What is your favorite *drink* **?** *Lemonade, of course!*

(pick something such as color, food, animal)

Activity #2.2

FREEZE FRAME

Students imagine their character's physical appearance.

NEED

- Completed **Goals, Motivation, and Conflict** graphic organizers (from Activity 1.5)
- Drawing paper (one per student)
- Crayons or colored pencils
- **Freeze Frame** graphic organizer (one per student)
- **Checklists for Freeze Frame** (one per student)

TIME: 45 MINUTES

- 30 minutes to draw/describe characters
- 15 minutes for follow up sharing and discussion

COMMON CORE ANCHOR STANDARDS

WRITING:

W.3 Write narratives to develop real or imagined experiences or events using effective technique, well-chosen details and well-structured event sequences.

LANGUAGE:

L.3 Apply knowledge of language to understand how language functions in different contexts, to make effective choices for meaning or style, and to comprehend more fully when reading or listening.

WHAT TO DO

1 Talk to your students about the need to clearly visualize what their characters look like. Having a clear picture of a character's physical appearance is extremely helpful to an author for several reasons. First, being able to "see" a character allows for better descriptions. Is your main character's hair strawberry blond, dirty blond, golden blond, or bleached blond with purple highlights? A picture may help make this decision. Second, once you've chosen that shade of blond, you don't want to write a description that isn't in keeping with that color. For example, you don't want to say her hair is like a field of golden wheat in one spot in your story, and then describe it as neon yellow in another place. A picture is good for remembering eye color, skin complexion, nose shape, and other important physical features. It ensures consistency, and consistency creates believability.

2 Give students a blank sheet of drawing paper. Tell them to close their eyes and think of

the character they developed on the **Goals, Motivation, and Conflict** graphic organizer. Have them imagine that the character is walking toward them. When the character gets close enough for students to see the details of his/her/its face and body, have students "freeze the frame" and draw everything they see about their characters. This picture should be a head to toe (or tail, as the case may be) image in color.

3 When the pictures are done, suggest that students label important things they want to remember when writing about this character. For example, they might label a character's sweatshirt pocket with "keeps chewing gum in here at all times," or a baseball cap with "her father gave her this on her tenth birthday, right before he left for good." These little notes may help students discover deeper layers of their characters.

4 Display the pictures in the classroom where the students can study them during free moments. Students will be writing while not actually writing, because a part of their brains will be considering those characters they see. When it is time to sit down and write, the words will come, because lots of thinking about the characters has been done without the students even knowing it.

5 Students can extend this drawing exercise by filling in the **Freeze Frame** graphic organizer with words and phrases they can use in their stories. They should look at their pictures for inspiration. Encourage specific and vivid word choice.

ASSESSMENT

Students' finished pictures can be assessed according to the level of detail given to the characters using the **Checklists for Freeze Frame**. The **Freeze Frame** graphic organizer can also be used as an evaluation.

Name: ______________________ Date: __________

Freeze Frame

DIRECTIONS

Fill in the circles with specific words and interesting phrases to describe your character's physical appearance. Look at your drawing of the character to help.

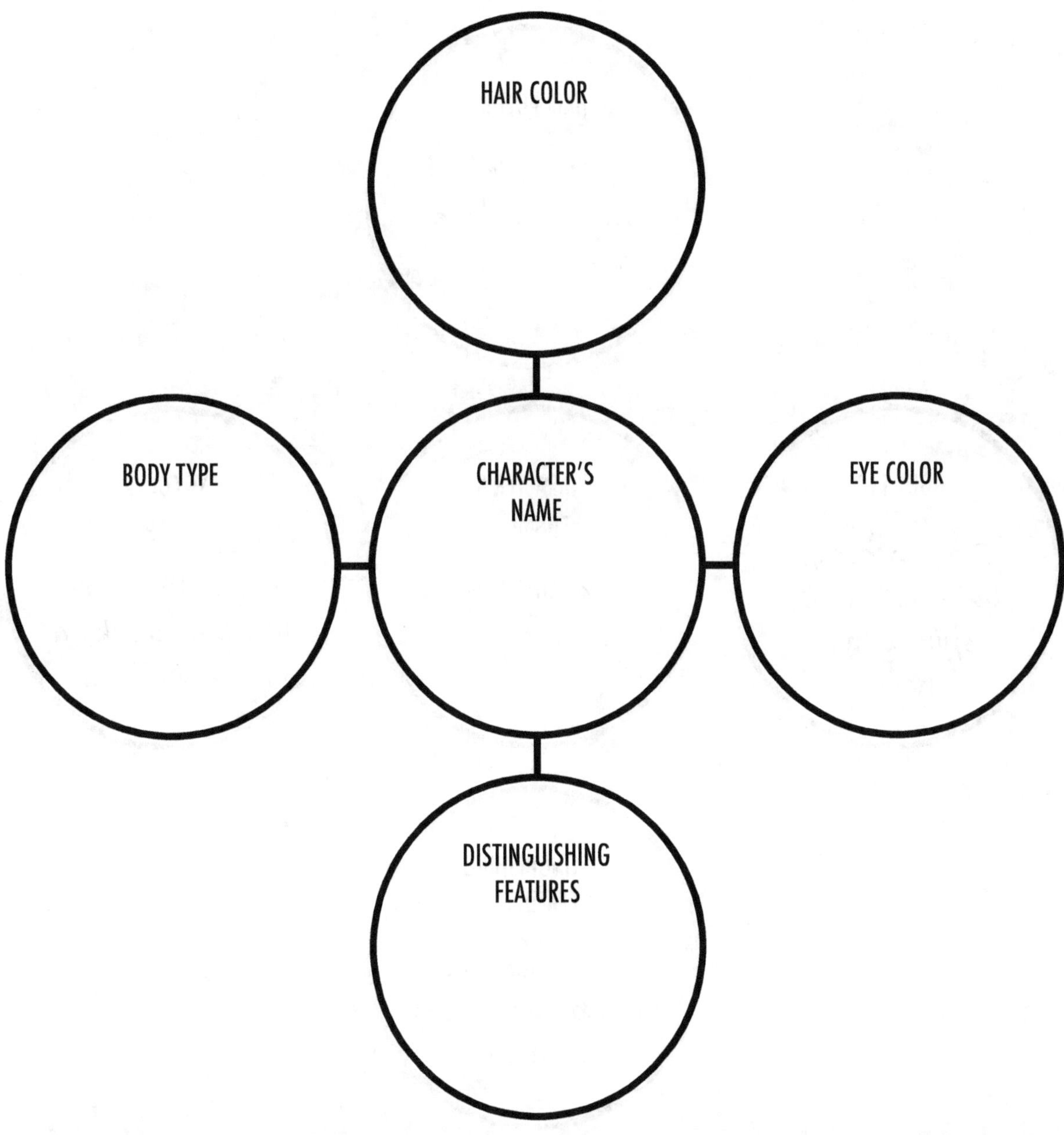

Name: ____________________ Date: ____________

Freeze Frame

DIRECTIONS

Fill in the circles with specific words and interesting phrases to describe your character's physical appearance. Look at your drawing of the character to help.

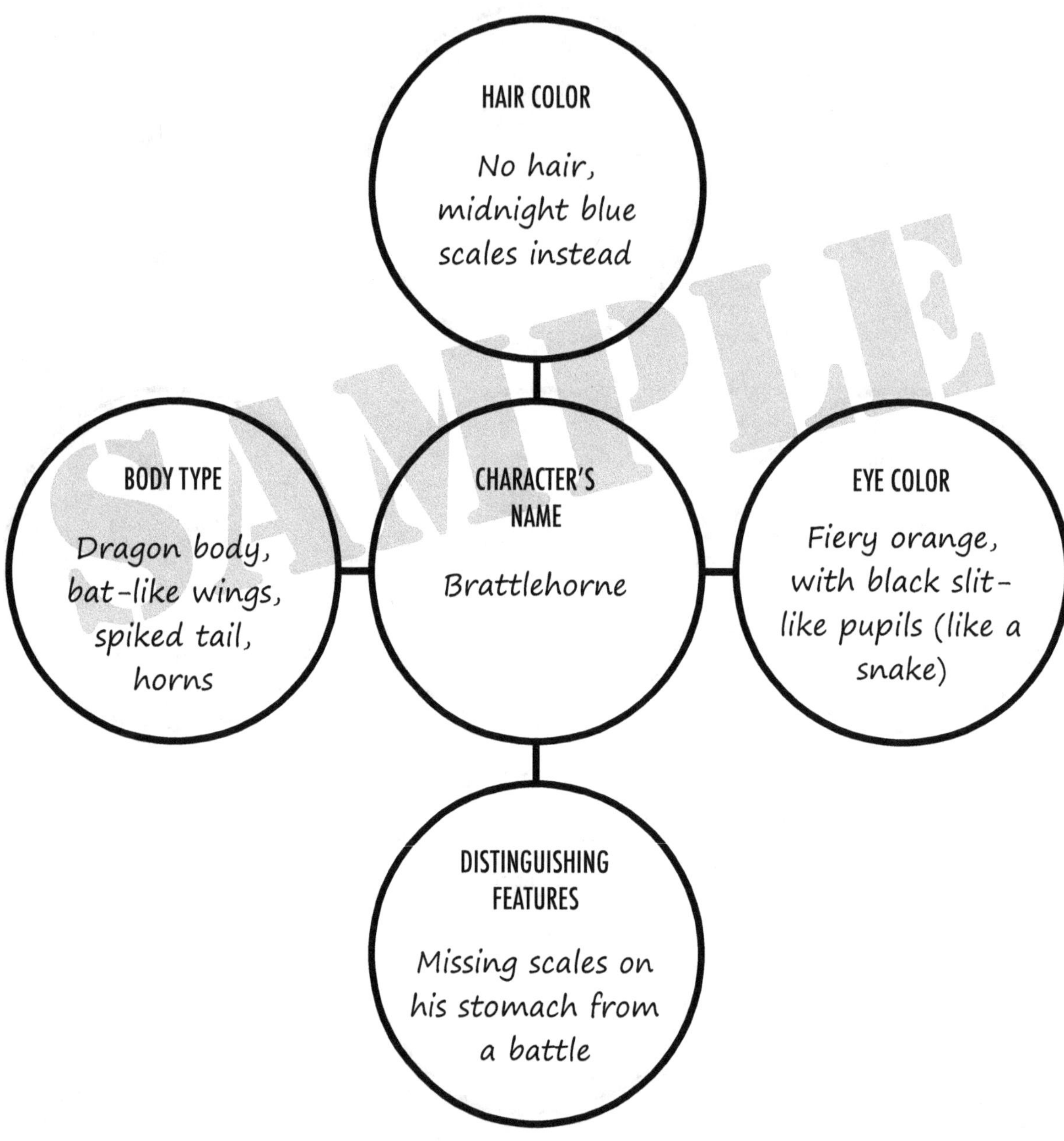

Freeze Frame

FREEZE FRAME	FREEZE FRAME
Student Name: ____________ Date: ____________ ☐ Picture is well-constructed with pertinent details represented. ☐ "Notes" have been left around the picture to give the character depth. ☐ A link between character traits and physical appearance has been established. Comments: ____________	Student Name: ____________ Date: ____________ ☐ Picture is well-constructed with pertinent details represented. ☐ "Notes" have been left around the picture to give the character depth. ☐ A link between character traits and physical appearance has been established. Comments: ____________
FREEZE FRAME	**FREEZE FRAME**
Student Name: ____________ Date: ____________ ☐ Picture is well-constructed with pertinent details represented. ☐ "Notes" have been left around the picture to give the character depth. ☐ A link between character traits and physical appearance has been established. Comments: ____________	Student Name: ____________ Date: ____________ ☐ Picture is well-constructed with pertinent details represented. ☐ "Notes" have been left around the picture to give the character depth. ☐ A link between character traits and physical appearance has been established. Comments: ____________
FREEZE FRAME	**FREEZE FRAME**
Student Name: ____________ Date: ____________ ☐ Picture is well-constructed with pertinent details represented. ☐ "Notes" have been left around the picture to give the character depth. ☐ A link between character traits and physical appearance has been established. Comments: ____________	Student Name: ____________ Date: ____________ ☐ Picture is well-constructed with pertinent details represented. ☐ "Notes" have been left around the picture to give the character depth. ☐ A link between character traits and physical appearance has been established. Comments: ____________

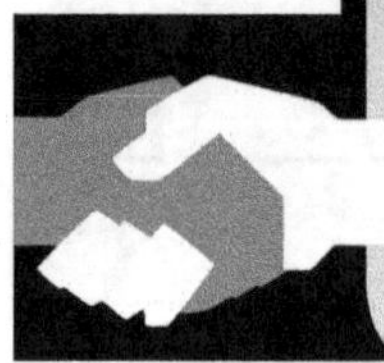

Activity #2.3

CHARACTER INTERVIEW

Students use the character interview technique with the character they are creating.

NEED

- **Character Interview** graphic organizers (one per student)
- **Checklists for Character Interview** (one per student)

TIME: 45 MINUTES

- 30 minutes to interview character
- 15 minutes follow-up sharing and discussion

COMMON CORE ANCHOR STANDARDS

WRITING:

W.3 Write narratives to develop real or imagined experiences or events using effective technique, well-chosen details and well-structured event sequences.

LANGUAGE:

L.3 Apply knowledge of language to understand how language functions in different contexts, to make effective choices for meaning or style, and to comprehend more fully when reading or listening.

WHAT TO DO

1. Instruct students to find a quiet spot away from each other. If the weather allows, take them outside so they can really spread out. Being outside reminds writers to use all the senses when writing.
2. Once they've located a suitable working spot, give students a blank **Character Interview** graphic organizer. Don't give many directions. The results are better when students just go for it. Let them know that they might not use all the questions, but they should try to consider each one through the eyes of their character.
3. Allow ample time for these interviews. They may take more than one class period, but it will be time well spent. If students have a difficult time getting started, suggest they go for a walk with their character. When our bodies are engaged in the simple act of walking, our brains can reach a highly creative level. While walking, students may encounter other people who in turn may spark ideas for the character.
4. After students complete the **Character Interview** graphic organizers, have them share with a partner. Partners should listen closely and offer any feedback that will help improve the character.

5 Students should save the interviews in a writing folder. They may never use anything from this sheet in their actual story, but this exercise will help them get to know their characters so well that writing about them is going to be a breeze. If they get stuck while composing the story, these interviews are helpful in getting un-stuck.

My characters speak loudest to me when I'm out in my neighborhood, walking my wolf of a German Shepherd and listening to my favorite music. When I've told students to go on such a walk, they often look at me with the "Are you serious?" face. I hand them a small notebook and a pencil and tell them to write down whatever their characters say on the walk. I've never had a student come back with an empty notebook. Never.

ASSESSMENT

Use the **Checklists for Character Interview** to assess students on this activity. Be sure to give these **Character Interviews** back to students as soon as possible. They will need them when they are ready to write their stories.

Name: ______________________ Date: __________

Character Interview

DIRECTIONS

Answer the following questions as if you were your character. Try to be as detailed as you can. You may add questions you think are important for your character to answer.

What is your name?

____

How old are you?

____

Where do you live?

____

Who is in your family?

____

Do you have any pets? If so, what kinds?

____

What do you like to do?

____

What annoys you?

____

What are your dreams?

____

What do you fear?

____

Who is your best friend?

____

How would your best friend describe you?

____

Where do you go when you want to be alone?

____

Name: ______________________ Date: ____________

Character Interview — Page 2

What makes you laugh out loud?

____

What makes you cry?

____

Which talent would you most like to have?

____

What is your favorite saying? (This could be a quote, catch phrase, or motto.)

____

____

What is your favorite food?

____

What is your favorite book?

____

What is your favorite movie?

____

What is your favorite season?

____

What kind of clothes are you most comfortable in?

____

What is your biggest problem?

____

____

Who do you go to for advice?

____

Other questions:

____

____

____

Name: ______________________ Date: ______________

Character Interview

DIRECTIONS

Answer the following questions as if you were your character. Try to be as detailed as you can. You may add questions you think are important for your character to answer.

What is your name?

Squiggles, the kitten

How old are you?

4 months old

Where do you live?

Right now under the McReynold's porch.

Who is in your family?

Just me. We all scattered when the black boots came along.

Do you have any pets? If so, what kinds?

No, but I'd love to be someone else's pet. Maybe Jenny's who lives across the street.

What do you like to do?

Chase mice, climb trees, take naps, play, but I don't have anyone to play with.

What annoys you?

Dogs, who bark at me for no reason. Children, who think it's funny to scare me.

What are your dreams?

To find an owner that wants me.

What do you fear?

Being alone.

Who is your best friend?

Jay, a bluejay.

How would your best friend describe you?

Furry and clumsy.

Where do you go when you want to be alone?

I never want to be alone. But I'm always alone under the porch.

Name: ____________________ Date: ____________

Character Interview — Page 2

What makes you laugh out loud?

Jay, when he tries to fit on the birdfeeder in the McReynold's yard. He's too big for it.

What makes you cry?

The long, cold night.

Which talent would you most like to have?

The talent to make someone want me.

What is your favorite saying? (This could be a quote, catch phrase, or motto.)

"Maybe tomorrow." Jay says I say this all the time. He doesn't make it sound like a good thing.

What is your favorite food?

Tuna

What is your favorite book?

I don't know how to read.

What is your favorite movie?

Puss in Boots

What is your favorite season?

Spring

What kind of clothes are you most comfortable in?

Cats do not like clothes. Ever!

What is your biggest problem?

That I don't have an owner and this is the coldest winter on record. It is not warm under this porch at all. I'm freezing, hungry, and tired.

Who do you go to for advice?

Jay, but he doesn't understand how badly I want to be Jenny's cat.

Other questions:

____

____

____

Character Interview

CHARACTER INTERVIEW	CHARACTER INTERVIEW
Student Name: ______________ Date: ______________ ☐ Student has detailed answers to the interview questions. ☐ Answers show creativity. ☐ Answers show a deep understanding of the character. ☐ Character has multiple layers. Comments: ______________ ______________	Student Name: ______________ Date: ______________ ☐ Student has detailed answers to the interview questions. ☐ Answers show creativity. ☐ Answers show a deep understanding of the character. ☐ Character has multiple layers. Comments: ______________ ______________
CHARACTER INTERVIEW	**CHARACTER INTERVIEW**
Student Name: ______________ Date: ______________ ☐ Student has detailed answers to the interview questions. ☐ Answers show creativity. ☐ Answers show a deep understanding of the character. ☐ Character has multiple layers. Comments: ______________ ______________	Student Name: ______________ Date: ______________ ☐ Student has detailed answers to the interview questions. ☐ Answers show creativity. ☐ Answers show a deep understanding of the character. ☐ Character has multiple layers. Comments: ______________ ______________
CHARACTER INTERVIEW	**CHARACTER INTERVIEW**
Student Name: ______________ Date: ______________ ☐ Student has detailed answers to the interview questions. ☐ Answers show creativity. ☐ Answers show a deep understanding of the character. ☐ Character has multiple layers. Comments: ______________ ______________	Student Name: ______________ Date: ______________ ☐ Student has detailed answers to the interview questions. ☐ Answers show creativity. ☐ Answers show a deep understanding of the character. ☐ Character has multiple layers. Comments: ______________ ______________

Activity #2.4

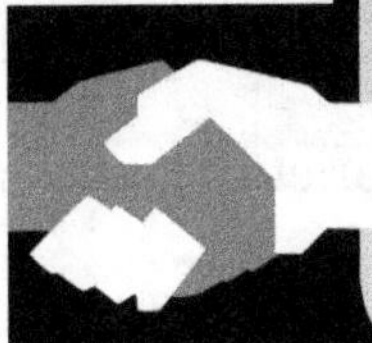

HABITAT

Consider the places where the student's character spends time.

NEED

- Drawing paper (one per student)
- Writer's Notebooks

TIME: 45 MINUTES

- 30 minutes to describe characters' habitats
- 15 minutes follow-up sharing and discussion

COMMON CORE ANCHOR STANDARDS

WRITING:

W.3 Write narratives to develop real or imagined experiences or events using effective technique, well-chosen details and well-structured event sequences.

LANGUAGE:

L.3 Apply knowledge of language to understand how language functions in different contexts, to make effective choices for meaning or style, and to comprehend more fully when reading or listening.

WHAT TO DO

1 Students sketch a labeled blueprint of the character's main setting on a piece of drawing paper. It could be a bedroom, a cave, a forest, a school gymnasium, an extraterrestrial spacecraft, or whatever suits the developed character. This doesn't have to be a superb piece of artwork. A quick illustration showing the contents of the setting and items important to the character is all that is needed.

2 Students share their drawings with a partner when they are finished. Partners should ask each other at least one meaningful question about their pictures.

QUESTIONS TO ASK STUDENTS

Why did you pick this setting to draw?

Why is ______________________________

(name something in the picture) important to your character?

Who would your character let into this place?

EXTEND THIS ACTIVITY

For students who finish quickly, ask them to respond in their Writer's Notebooks to one of the following questions:

- What is in your character's backpack, suitcase, purse, gym bag, briefcase, etc?
- What is in your character's refrigerator?
- What is in your character's garbage can?
- What kinds of things does your character save?
- What would your character do on a Friday night? Saturday morning? Sunday afternoon?

ASSESSMENT

Students' finished drawings and written responses in Writer's Notebooks can be used as assessment pieces.

HABITAT

Sample Entry in Writer's Notebook

Habitat – My Character's Backpack

Jackson's backpack is where he keeps everything he needs. A flashlight for reading comics late at night. His iPod for tunes whenever he wants them. A notebook and Spiderman pencil for writing down Important Ideas and doodling. A seashell from the beach he went to with his mom on vacation last summer. It reminds him of his mom who he doesn't get to see as much anymore. Six dollars, for emergencies. A granola bar, even though Cheryl, his dad's girlfriend, doesn't get the good kind. A pair of black 1980s sunglasses he found in his dad's desk drawer. A note Courtney Remines passed him in math class two days ago. "Do u like me?" it read. He still hasn't written back. A baseball card of some player he never heard of, but his uncle went nuts over. And finally, a travel-sized version of his favorite game, Battleship.

Activity #2.5

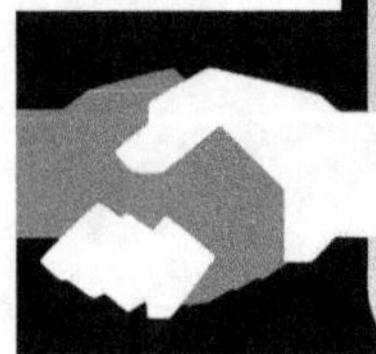

TREASURE BOX

This activity allows students to think more deeply about their characters by describing items of importance to the characters.

NEED

- **Treasure Box** graphic organizer (one per student)

TIME: 35 MINUTES

- 20 minutes to write about characters' items
- 15 minutes follow-up sharing and discussion

COMMON CORE ANCHOR STANDARDS

WRITING:

W.3 Write narratives to develop real or imagined experiences or events using effective technique, well-chosen details and well-structured event sequences.

LANGUAGE:

L.3 Apply knowledge of language to understand how language functions in different contexts, to make effective choices for meaning or style, and to comprehend more fully when reading or listening.

WHAT TO DO

1. Ask students to think about one personal item that is very special to their characters. Students complete the **Treasure Box** graphic organizer. They can sketch the item or put a photo of it on the graphic organizer, but the bulk of the time should be spent on using words to describe the item and what it means to the character.
2. When all students are finished, have them meet in groups of four or five to share their characters' items and reasons for keeping them.

ASSESSMENT

Finished **Treasure Box** graphic organizers can be used as assessment pieces.

Name: ______________________ Date: __________

Treasure Box

DIRECTIONS

Clearly describe one personal item that is important to your character. Sketch it in the box or paste a photo, and then answer the questions.

QUESTIONS

What is the item? ______________________

____

Where did your character get the item? ______________________

____

Why has your character decided to save this item? ______________________

____

What would your character be willing to do to keep this item safe? ______________________

____

How would your character feel if something happened to this item? ______________________

____

Name: ______________________ Date: __________

Treasure Box

DIRECTIONS

Clearly describe one personal item that is important to your character. Sketch it in the box or paste a photo, and then answer the questions.

QUESTIONS

What is the item? A dragonfly necklace, silver with amethyst crystals on the body

Where did your character get the item? Her grandmother who always said dragonflies were good luck

Why has your character decided to save this item? Grammy said it would be important some day

What would your character be willing to do to keep this item safe? Anything. Shelby already keeps it in a super secret spot. Somewhere where no one, not even her sneaky little brother, Tommy, will find it.

How would your character feel if something happened to this item? She would be heartbroken, like she lost Grammy all over again.

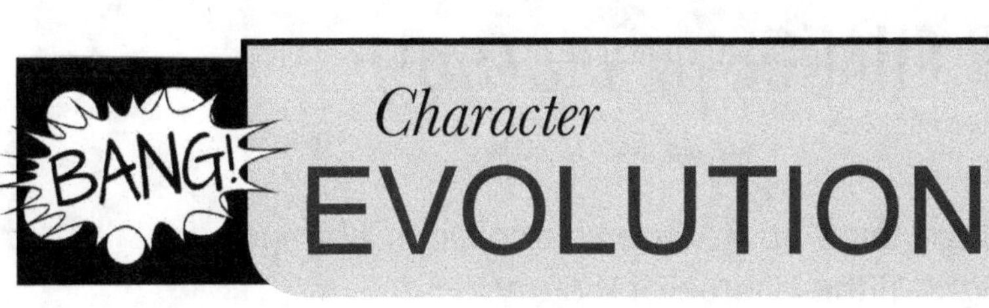

Character EVOLUTION

3

People change. They go through phases, grow, fail, and succeed. Fictional characters need to do the same.

People change. They go through phases, grow, fail, and succeed. Fictional characters need to do the same.

Tell your students to think of the most recent piece of fiction they have read or the last television drama or movie they have watched. Zoom in on the main character. What was he/she/it like at the beginning of the book, show, or movie? At the end? What events shaped who the character became by the end of the story? What was the turning point that started the change for this character?

If characters didn't change throughout the course of a story, they'd be boring to read about. Readers crave the action that happens when cause-and-effect events occur and force the characters to adjust in some fashion. This is how a character blossoms and learns. It is up to the author to show that transformation. Without change and flaws, characters can seem two-dimensional and stagnant. Only by giving them layers, forcing them to react to situations, and making them question themselves and the events they are involved in can writers truly make their characters leap off the page.

Your students know their characters well at this point. Now they are ready to think about how their characters will change throughout the course of the stories they will write. Make it clear to your students that character evolution doesn't just apply to the main character or the hero. Villains may be mischievous at the start of a story and reach full-blown evilness, or a villain may have a change of heart by the end of a story. Supporting characters often change, too. All characters evolve in some way.

IN THIS CHAPTER:

ACTIVITY 3.1: As a class, examine how a published character changes throughout a story.

ACTIVITY 3.2: In pairs, examine how another published character changes throughout a story.

ACTIVITY 3.3: Plan how the students' own fictional characters will undergo change.

ACTIVITY 3.4: Examine beliefs and flaws of published characters.

ACTIVITY 3.5: Develop beliefs and flaws for the characters students are creating.

Activity #3.1

CHARACTER CHANGE *(WHOLE CLASS)*

As a class, students examine how a known character changes throughout the course of a story.

NEED

- **Character Change** graphic organizers (one per student)
- **Character Traits** sheet (page 20)

TIME: 45 MINUTES

- 30 minutes to analyze character change
- 15 minutes follow-up sharing and discussion

SUGGESTED TEXTS

Verdi, by Janell Cannon

COMMON CORE ANCHOR STANDARDS

WRITING:
W.3 Write narratives to develop real or imagined experiences or events using effective technique, well-chosen details and well-structured event sequences.

LANGUAGE:
L.3 Apply knowledge of language to understand how language functions in different contexts, to make effective choices for meaning or style, and to comprehend more fully when reading or listening.

READING:
RL.3 Describe in depth a character, setting, or event in a story or drama, drawing on specific details in the text (e.g., a character's thoughts, words, or actions).

WHAT TO DO

1. Guide students through this activity after reading a picture book aloud to the class. *Verdi*, by Janell Cannon, is a great choice. It is the story of a snake who doesn't want to turn from a fun, sporty yellow to a dull, boring green. Essentially, he doesn't want to grow up. The story is simple and quick, and the character exhibits change very clearly, so students can see it happening. Any book or excerpt with a dynamic character will illustrate character change for students.
2. After reading the picture book, display the **Character Change** graphic organizer to the class. Guide students through the sheet for the snake character in *Verdi*. Work as a class to fill in the organizer together. By studying the work of the experts, students will be exposed to well-developed characters that change.

QUESTIONS TO ASK STUDENTS

What is the character like at the beginning of the story? Can we use a one-word character trait to describe him/her/it?

What is the character like at the end of the story? Can we use a one-word character trait to describe him/her/it?

What events show what he/she/it is like at beginning? (Fill the first two boxes with events that highlight the beginning-of-story trait.)

What is the turning point event that started the change? (Fill in the middle box labeled "Turning Point" with this event.)

What events show what he/she/it is like at the end? (Fill the last two boxes with events that highlight the end-of-story trait.)

The completed **Character Change** graphic organizer should clearly illustrate how the main character has evolved throughout the course of the story and indicate what events the author has used to show that change. Point out that the author never *told* readers that the character was something at the beginning and then something different at the end. Instead, the author *showed* readers through events and the character's actions, thoughts, and words. Once again, *show*, not *tell*.

ASSESSMENT

Informal assessment can occur as students participate in filling in the class **Character Change** graphic organizer.

Name: ______________________ Date: ______________

Character Change

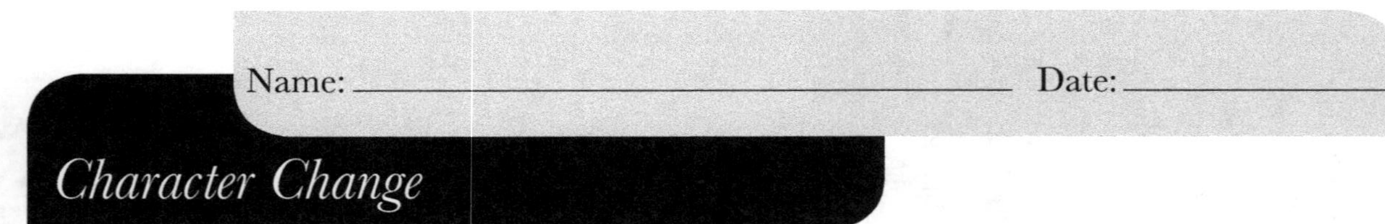

DIRECTIONS

Fill in the "At the beginning" and "At the end" boxes with one-word character traits to describe what the character is like at the beginning and end of the story. Then place events in the flow chart to show how the character changes throughout the course of the story.

CHARACTER'S NAME: ______________________ **TITLE OF STORY:** ______________________

At the beginning...

At the end...

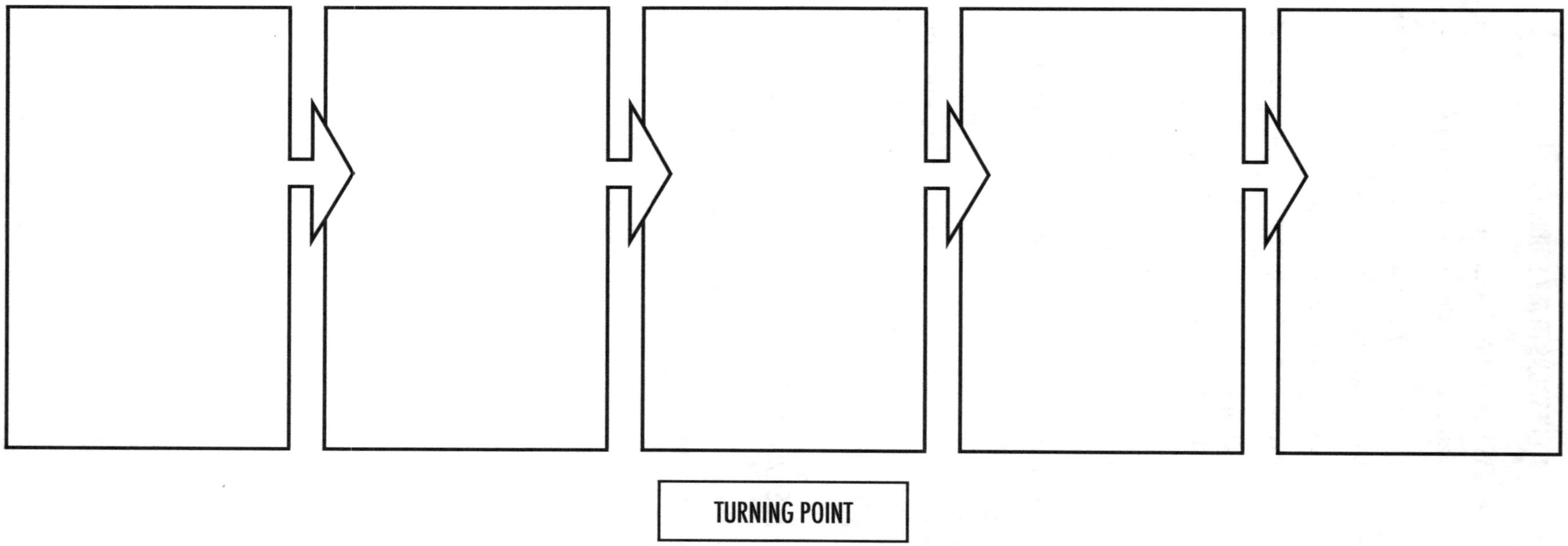

TURNING POINT

Name: ______________________ Date: ____________

Character Change

DIRECTIONS

Fill in the "At the beginning" and "At the end" boxes with one-word character traits to describe what the character is like at the beginning and end of the story. Then place events in the flow chart to show how the character changes throughout the course of the story.

CHARACTER'S NAME: *Verdi*

TITLE OF STORY: *Verdi*

At the beginning...

immature

At the end...

mature

Taps his tail/ interrupting the big green snakes

→ *Does crazy, dangerous tricks*

→ *Does a dizzying trick in the air, falls, and gets hurt*

TURNING POINT

→ *The big greens take care of Verdi, and he listens to their stories*

→ *Learns to be careful, but can still have fun and be himself*

Activity #3.2

CHARACTER CHANGE *(WITH PARTNERS)*

In pairs, students examine how a known character changes throughout the course of a story.

NEED

- **Character Change** graphic organizers, one per student (page 64)
- **Character Traits** sheets (page 20)
- Several picture books with strong characters

TIME: 45 MINUTES

- 30 minutes to complete **Character Change** graphic organizer
- 15 minutes follow-up sharing and discussion

SUGGESTED TEXTS

Stellaluna, by Janell Cannon
Albert, by Donna Jo Napoli
Fireflies, by Julie Brinckloe
Old Jake's Skirts, by Anne C. Scott

COMMON CORE ANCHOR STANDARDS

WRITING:
W.3 Write narratives to develop real or imagined experiences or events using effective technique, well-chosen details and well-structured event sequences.

LANGUAGE:
L.3 Apply knowledge of language to understand how language functions in different contexts, to make effective choices for meaning or style, and to comprehend more fully when reading or listening.

READING:
RL.3 Describe in depth a character, setting, or event in a story or drama, drawing on specific details in the text (e.g., a character's thoughts, words, or actions).

WHAT TO DO

1 Pair up the students and have them read a picture book with characters that clearly change as a result of their experiences in the story.

2 Student pairs complete one **Character Change** graphic organizer for the main character of that book. The **Character Traits** sheet will help students easily select words to describe the main character at the beginning and end of the story.

3 Pairs team up with another pair to share these examples of character change.

4 Choose a few to share with the whole class as a way to wrap up the activity.

ASSESSMENT

Completed **Character Change** graphic organizers can be used as assessment pieces.

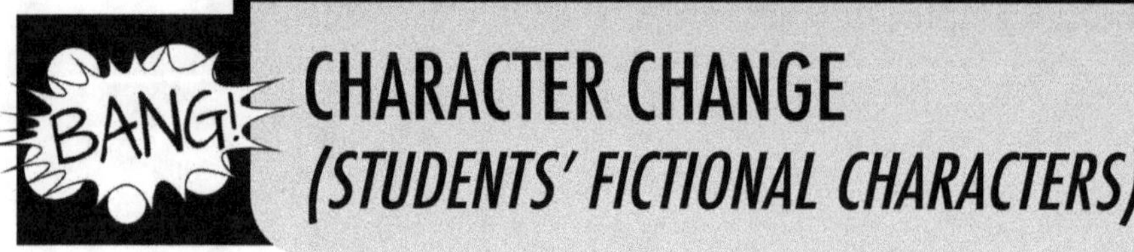

Activity #3.3

CHARACTER CHANGE (STUDENTS' FICTIONAL CHARACTERS)

Students plan how their own fictional character changes throughout the course of their story.

NEED

- **Character Change** graphic organizers, one per student (page 64)
- Completed **Goals, Motivation, and Conflict** graphic organizers (from Activity 1.5)
- **Character Traits** sheets (page 20)

TIME: 45 MINUTES

- 30 minutes to complete **Character Change** graphic organizer
- 15 minutes follow-up sharing and discussion

COMMON CORE ANCHOR STANDARDS

WRITING:

W.3 Write narratives to develop real or imagined experiences or events using effective technique, well-chosen details and well-structured event sequences.

LANGUAGE:

L.3 Apply knowledge of language to understand how language functions in different contexts, to make effective choices for meaning or style, and to comprehend more fully when reading or listening.

WHAT TO DO

1 Each student completes a **Character Change** graphic organizer for his/her main character. The process is the same as in the previous two activities, but now they assign the character traits they want their own fictional characters to display at the beginning and end of their stories. They can refer to the **Character Traits** sheet for assistance in picking beginning and ending traits. Students must consider the plots of their stories to create the events that will establish the beginning trait, the turning point event that will start the change, and the events that will illustrate the ending trait.

2 Confer with each student for a few moments as they grapple with completing this activity. Some will fly through it because their characters are so real to them. Others will stare blankly at the **Character Change** graphic organizer. Direct these students back to their completed **Goals, Motivation, and Conflict** sheets, their **Character Interviews**, and any other graphic organizers they have completed that may help. Encourage students to listen to their characters and choose events that seem natural.

TEACHER: *What is the turning point that changes your character from afraid to brave?*

STRUGGLING STUDENT: *My character will find a magic sword and a book of spells, fight a dragon, a giant squid, a three-headed cobra, and a man-eating mammoth. Then he'll go on a journey and meet a…"*

Sometimes struggling writing students will try to devise the most complex series of events in an overcompensating fashion. Recommend that they SIMPLIFY!

Too much! This student has enough ideas for five stories and needs to commit to one good idea. Students who aren't sure what to do sometimes want to do it all, or they swipe plots from stories they know and try to put them all together. The end result is a series of events that don't flow smoothly and a character who hasn't really achieved anything. Suggest simplifying the story so that one event is the turning point. The first two events should logically lead to the turning point, and the last two events should lead to the resolution.

ASSESSMENT

Use the **Checklists for Character Change** to assess students on their work.

Character Change

CHARACTER CHANGE	CHARACTER CHANGE
Student Name: ________ Date: ________ ☐ Opposing character traits have been chosen to show change throughout the story. ☐ Events illustrate how the character will change. ☐ Turning point event forces the character to change and makes sense within the context of the story. Comments: ________	Student Name: ________ Date: ________ ☐ Opposing character traits have been chosen to show change throughout the story. ☐ Events illustrate how the character will change. ☐ Turning point event forces the character to change and makes sense within the context of the story. Comments: ________
CHARACTER CHANGE	**CHARACTER CHANGE**
Student Name: ________ Date: ________ ☐ Opposing character traits have been chosen to show change throughout the story. ☐ Events illustrate how the character will change. ☐ Turning point event forces the character to change and makes sense within the context of the story. Comments: ________	Student Name: ________ Date: ________ ☐ Opposing character traits have been chosen to show change throughout the story. ☐ Events illustrate how the character will change. ☐ Turning point event forces the character to change and makes sense within the context of the story. Comments: ________
CHARACTER CHANGE	**CHARACTER CHANGE**
Student Name: ________ Date: ________ ☐ Opposing character traits have been chosen to show change throughout the story. ☐ Events illustrate how the character will change. ☐ Turning point event forces the character to change and makes sense within the context of the story. Comments: ________	Student Name: ________ Date: ________ ☐ Opposing character traits have been chosen to show change throughout the story. ☐ Events illustrate how the character will change. ☐ Turning point event forces the character to change and makes sense within the context of the story. Comments: ________

Activity #3.4

CHARACTER BELIEFS AND BAD HABITS/FLAWS *(WITH PARTNERS)*

Students examine a published character beliefs about him or herself or about the world and consider the character's bad habits and flaws.

NEED

- **Character Beliefs and Bad Habits/Flaws** graphic organizers (one per student)
- **Character Traits** sheet (page 20)

TIME: 45 MINUTES

- 30 minutes to complete **Character Beliefs and Bad Habits/Flaws** graphic organizer
- 15 minutes follow-up sharing and discussion

SUGGESTED TEXTS

See Suggested Texts chart (pages 94-95)

COMMON CORE ANCHOR STANDARDS

WRITING:

W.3 Write narratives to develop real or imagined experiences or events using effective technique, well-chosen details and well-structured event sequences.

LANGUAGE:

L.3 Apply knowledge of language to understand how language functions in different contexts, to make effective choices for meaning or style, and to comprehend more fully when reading or listening.

READING:

RL.3 Describe in depth a character, setting, or event in a story or drama, drawing on specific details in the text (e.g., a character's thoughts, words, or actions).

WHAT TO DO

1 Start by explaining that characters often misinterpret the situations they are in, and readers keep reading to find out if these perceptions will be cleared up by the story's end. For example: Harry Potter and Percy Jackson believe they are normal boys. Evan Treski in *The Lemonade War* thinks his sister is going to upstage him in fourth grade. Sal in *Walk Two Moons* believes she is going to find her mother. Aubrey in *Love, Aubrey* thinks if she continues with day-to-day routines, it's like her mother never left.

Also explain that characters have flaws and bad habits, just like real people. They bite their nails, obsess over their appearance, leave their toys all over the house, forget to put the toilet seat down, avoid talking about their feelings, steal things, abuse substances. These behaviors make characters more three-dimensional, more real, and sometimes contribute to the character change that happens over the course of the story.

2 Pair students together. Each pair chooses a character or is assigned a character from a book they have read.

3 Each student pair completes one **Character Beliefs and Bad Habits/Flaws** graphic organizer for the character. It should include one mistaken belief and one or two bad habits/flaws.

4 Point out to the students that a character often doesn't realize that his/her belief is mistaken and makes decisions based on that belief. The author usually drops subtle clues that the belief is a misunderstanding or the result of an experience the character has had. Students may need assistance in inferring a mistaken belief. If so, pull excerpts from the text students are working with.

QUESTIONS TO ASK STUDENTS

Why would the character make this decision?

Why does the character feel this way?

What past experiences has the character had that would make them believe what they do?

Is this belief meant to protect the character from getting hurt emotionally? How?

5 When the graphic organizers are completed, students share their responses with another pair.

ASSESSMENT

Completed **Character Beliefs and Bad Habits/Flaws** graphic organizers can be collected as assessment pieces.

Name: ______________________ Date: __________

Character Beliefs and Bad Habits/Flaws

DIRECTIONS

Fill in the chart below with at least one belief your character has about himself/herself/itself or about how the world works. Also include one or two bad habits/flaws for your character. Remember, beliefs and bad habits/flaws should be directly related to the plot of your story.

CHARACTER BELIEF	CHARACTER BAD HABITS/FLAWS

Name: ______________________________ Date: ______________

Character Beliefs and Bad Habits/Flaws

DIRECTIONS

Fill in the chart below with at least one belief your character has about himself/herself/itself or about how the world works. Also include one or two bad habits/flaws for your character. Remember, beliefs and bad habits/flaws should be directly related to the plot of your story.

CHARACTER BELIEF	CHARACTER BAD HABITS/FLAWS
Remy believes he is cursed and will never be successful at anything.	*Remy cracks his knuckles when he is nervous.* *Remy quits before he really gives anything his full effort. If it even looks like he might fail, he walks away.*

Activity #3.5

CHARACTER BELIEFS AND BAD HABITS/FLAWS *(STUDENTS' FICTIONAL CHARACTERS)*

Students develop their own fictional characters' beliefs and bad habits/flaws.

NEED

- **Character Beliefs and Bad Habits/Flaws** graphic organizers, one per student (page 73)
- Completed **Goals, Motivation, and Conflict** graphic organizers (from Activity 1.5)
- **Character Traits** sheet (page 20)

TIME: 45 MINUTES

- 30 minutes to complete **Character Beliefs and Bad Habits/Flaws** graphic organizers
- 15 minutes follow-up sharing and discussion

COMMON CORE ANCHOR STANDARDS

WRITING:

W.3 Write narratives to develop real or imagined experiences or events using effective technique, well-chosen details and well-structured event sequences.

LANGUAGE:

L.3 Apply knowledge of language to understand how language functions in different contexts, to make effective choices for meaning or style, and to comprehend more fully when reading or listening.

WHAT TO DO

1 Each student completes the **Character Beliefs and Bad Habits/Flaws** graphic organizer for one character he/she is creating. Students should include one mistaken belief and one or two bad habits/flaws. Remind students that beliefs and bad habits/flaws should be directly related to the plot of their stories.

2 When the graphic organizers are completed, students share their responses with a partner. Partners listen to determine if the belief and bad habits/flaws seem realistic to the type of character being created.

3 Circulate to check in with student pairs. Review their completed graphic organizers. Offer feedback where necessary.

4 Students revise as needed based on partner and teacher feedback.

ASSESSMENT

Completed **Character Beliefs and Bad Habits/Flaws** graphic organizers can be collected as assessment pieces.

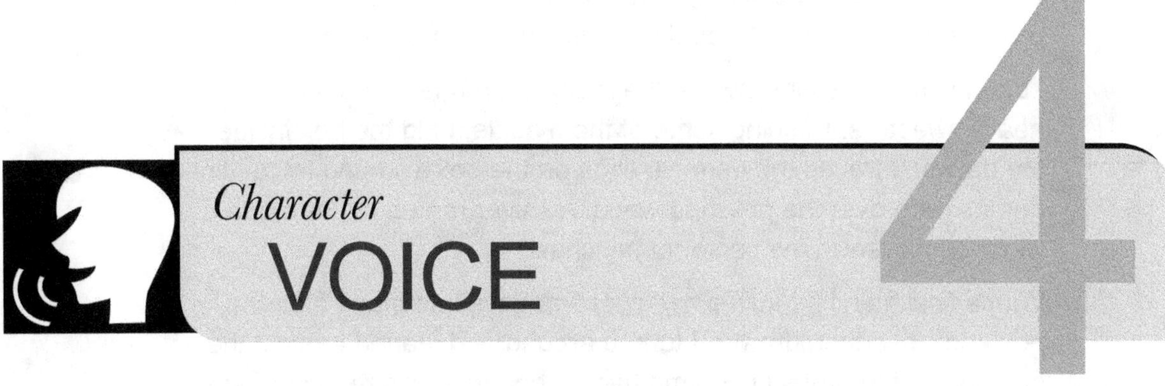

Character VOICE

Consider the people you know. Do they all sound the same? Of course not. Your next-door neighbor likes to swear. Your cousin laughs like a hyena. Your best friend says everything at a secretive whisper. Your college roommate from Paris spoke with a French accent. These different voices help define characters. Readers are exposed to voice through dialogue between characters as well as a particular author's style and tone of writing.

Author's voice and character's voice work together to bring an individual flavor to each work of fiction. Students often struggle to find their author's voice, but it is never too early to help them cultivate a consistent voice in their writing. Character's voice comes to students a little easier because they can be encouraged to put themselves in the character's shoes. Trying on different voices is fun, too, and invites students to explore saying things in ways they wouldn't normally say them.

The best way to learn about voice is to listen to different voices in everyday life. Writers often fill many pages in their Writer's Notebooks with fragments of overheard conversations because something about the way things were said intrigued them. I remember being in a home improvement store where the cashier caught my attention. I overheard her talking and immediately dug out my writing notebook. In the span of five minutes, I scribbled down the following:

"Holy Hannah-Banana!"
"And you're off like a kitten. Have a great day."
"Well, you're a pistol, ain't ya?"
"Hell-ooo, Kitty! Whatcha buyin' today?"

Her name tag said "Avaline." She was a fabulous, real live character and had a truly distinctive voice. She'd be the type of character that would leap off the pages of a book, grab you by the shirt collar, and make you listen to her. And you wouldn't be mixing her up with any other people in the story. That's what we want to encourage in students as they create their own characters.

Activity 4.4 helps students understand the concept of point of view when building their characters. Point of view plays a starring role in developing characters and giving them a voice. Students need to consider what point of view will work best for their story—first or third person.

Introduce the concept of point of view with a whole-class discussion, using examples to show the difference between first person and third person points of view.

Read the following excerpt as an example of first person point of view:

> I held the wooden box tightly in my hands. Mama would never forgive me if I dropped it. I wouldn't forgive me if I dropped it.

> I held the wooden box tightly in my hands. Mama would never forgive me if I dropped it. I wouldn't forgive me if I dropped it.
>
> I opened my dresser drawer—the really deep one that held all my heavy sweaters. Pushing some of them aside, I hid the box inside the drawer. I traced the dark carvings on the box's lid and let my fingertips glide over the polished wood. A shiver ran up my arm and a warm spot grew in the center of my chest.
>
> With a final glance, I fluffed my sweaters back into place atop the box and closed the drawer. I turned around and leaned against the dresser as if to protect it. Mama hadn't thought I was ready for what was inside the box. Maybe she was right. It didn't matter now.
>
> I had the box.
>
> Its contents belonged to me.
>
> Only me.

Lead a brief discussion about how the piece uses the words *I, me,* and *my* extensively in the first person point of view, and how those words help a reader get inside the character's head. Students should notice such details as:

- You almost feel the box in your own hands.
- The uncertainty in the character sounds loud and clear.
- Her mother has doubts about her being ready for whatever is in the box, and she has the same doubts, yet you get a sense of pride over owning the box and its mysterious contents.

Students should understand that a great deal of information can be shown to the reader very subtly using first person point of view. Explain that first person point of view can be very successful if the plot mostly revolves around a *single* character.

Third person point of view distances the reader a bit, but it allows the author to share information about *many* characters. Readers get to experience multiple characters and see story events from different perspectives.

Read the following example of third person point of view:

> Chelsea held the wooden box tightly in her hands. "Now you take good care of this, Chelsea," Mama said. "I don't want it broken. It's very important to our family."
>
> Nodding, Chelsea walked upstairs to her bedroom and opened her dresser drawer—the really deep one that held all her heavy sweaters. Pushing some of them aside, she hid the box inside the drawer. She traced the dark carvings on the box's lid and let her fingertips glide over the polished wood. A shiver ran up Chelsea's arm and a warm spot grew in the center of her chest.

> "What's that?" Her brother, Joey, bounded into her room and reached a hand into the drawer.
>
> Chelsea slapped his hand away before he could reach the box. "None of your business!"
>
> Joey stuck his tongue out at her and stomped out of her room mumbling something about her being The Meanest Sister Ever.
>
> With a final glance at the box, Chelsea fluffed her sweaters back into place and closed the drawer. She turned around and leaned against the dresser as if to protect it. Her mama hadn't thought she was ready for what was inside the box, but it didn't matter now. Chelsea had the box. Its contents belonged to her.
>
> Only her.

Conduct another whole-class discussion about the difference between third and first person point of view. In third person, this piece now uses several characters' specific names and we get to see what is going on with all the characters, not just one. Students should notice such details as:

- hearing from all characters involved in the scene
- loss of the specific "inside" thoughts from one of the characters as in the first person point of view
- less emotional connection between reader and characters

Make sure students understand that both first and third person points of view work well. It's a matter of which will best hook the reader and achieve the goals of the story.

IN THIS CHAPTER:

ACTIVITY 4.1: Listen carefully and record the way real people talk.

ACTIVITY 4.2: Watch a television or movie character and determine how what he/she says develops his/her character.

ACTIVITY 4.3: Listen to a published character's "voice," and then write a short scene that develops a character's "voice."

ACTIVITY 4.4: Write parts of their stories in both first and third person points of view, and then work with other students to determine which point of view works best.

ACTIVITY 4.5: Explore different character perspectives and how they influence the development of voice.

Activity #4.1

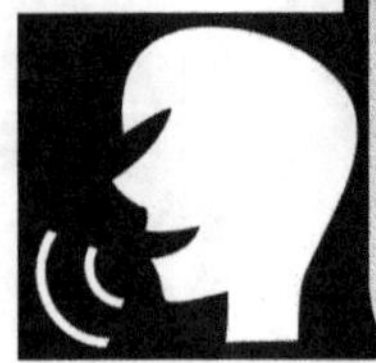

OPERATION: EAVESDROP

Understand the concept of voice by listening to the way real people talk and converse with one another.

NEED

- **Operation: Eavesdrop** graphic organizers (one or more per student)

TIME: HOMEWORK PLUS 15 MINUTES

- Several days to one week (homework) to collect examples of conversation
- 15 minutes for follow-up sharing and discussion in class

COMMON CORE ANCHOR STANDARDS

WRITING:

W.3 Write narratives to develop real or imagined experiences or events using effective technique, well-chosen details and well-structured event sequences.

LANGUAGE:

L.3 Apply knowledge of language to understand how language functions in different contexts, to make effective choices for meaning or style, and to comprehend more fully when reading or listening.

L.5 Demonstrate understanding of figurative language, word relationships, and nuances in word meanings.

WHAT TO DO

1. Give each student one or more **Operation: Eavesdrop** graphic organizers. Have students staple the graphic organizer into their Writer's Notebooks.
2. Explain to students that ideas for developing a character's voice can come from observations of people around them. Over the course of one week, students complete the graphic organizer by listening to conversations around them and collecting bits of conversation (nothing private or confidential, of course). Give students permission to eavesdrop. Tell them to keep their ears tuned in to what the people around them say and how they say it. Warn them not to pester anyone who doesn't want to be eavesdropped on. Encourage the collection of *interesting* lines. The "Hello, how are you?" conversations don't give us any creative spark.
3. When the week is over, have students share some lines they collected.

ASSESSMENT

Completed **Operation: Eavesdrop** graphic organizers can be collected as assessment pieces.

Encourage students to pay attention to voice in places where students might not normally listen, such as the grocery store. Both workers and shoppers are potential sources of great lines of dialogue.

Name: ____________________ Date: __________

Operation: Eavesdrop

DIRECTIONS

Listen to the people around you wherever you are. Pay close attention to what they say and how they say it. Collect some *interesting* lines of dialogue and record them. Include who said the lines and why, along with a quick, one-sentence physical description.

What was said

____

____

Who said it/Why

____

____

Physical Description

____

____

- - - - - - - - - - - - - - - - - -

What was said

____

____

Who said it/Why

____

____

Physical Description

____

____

Name: ______________________ Date: ______________

Operation: Eavesdrop

DIRECTIONS

Listen to the people around you wherever you are. Pay close attention to what they say and how they say it. Collect some *interesting* lines of dialogue and record them. Include who said the lines and why, along with a quick, one-sentence physical description.

What was said

This is the meanest sandwich I've ever eaten!

Who said it/Why

Nornie, my grandma, when she ate one of her own tasty eggplant sandwiches.

Physical Description

light blue pants, blue cardigan sweater over a flowered shirt, white sneakers, black and gray short hair, brown eyes, short

---

What was said

Where's that going?

Who said it/Why

My dad, when he built a wall in our basement and used a million nails. The wall didn't budge when he pushed on it.

Physical Description

short, black hair, beard, brown eyes, gray knit hat, gray thermal sweatshirt, stained jeans, brown work boots, tool belt, tall, strong

Activity #4.2

HE SAID, SHE SAID

Students examine examples of good character dialogue.

NEED

- **He Said, She Said** graphic organizers (one per student)

TIME: ONE HOMEWORK PLUS 15 MINUTES

- One afternoon/evening to study television/movie characters
- 15 minutes follow-up sharing and discussion the next day

COMMON CORE ANCHOR STANDARDS

WRITING:

W.3 Write narratives to develop real or imagined experiences or events using effective technique, well-chosen details and well-structured event sequences.

LANGUAGE:

L.3 Apply knowledge of language to understand how language functions in different contexts, to make effective choices for meaning or style, and to comprehend more fully when reading or listening.

L.5 Demonstrate understanding of figurative language, word relationships, and nuances in word meanings.

WHAT TO DO

1. Ask students to watch their favorite television show or movie. (Yes, they'll hate this.)
2. Students complete the **He Said, She Said** graphic organizer while they watch a favorite character. They can choose any character for this activity, because all characters should have unique voices to study.
3. Students meet in small groups of four or five to discuss the character voices they examined.

QUESTIONS TO ASK STUDENTS

What did the writer of the show/movie do successfully with this character's voice?

What physical movements added to this character's voice?

What did you learn about voice by studying this character?

ASSESSMENT

Completed **He Said, She Said** graphic organizers can be collected as assessment pieces.

Name: ____________________ Date: __________

He Said, She Said

DIRECTIONS

Watch your favorite television show or movie. Study one of the characters very closely and answer the following questions for that character. Be specific.

Who is the character you are studying?

____

Provide a sample of something this character says during the show/movie.

____

____

____

What does that sample tell you about the character?

____

____

____

Does this character have a catch phrase? What is it?

____

____

How does this character react to other characters?

____

____

If you were to have a phone conversation with this character, what would it sound like?

____

____

Name: ______________________ Date: ____________

He Said, She Said

DIRECTIONS

Watch your favorite TV show or movie. Study one of the characters very closely and answer the following questions for that character. Be specific.

Who is the character you are studying?

Flynn Rider from the movie Tangled.

Provide a sample of something this character says during the show/movie.

"I could get used to a view like this. Yep, I'm used to it. Guys, I want a castle."

"So! Hey can I ask you something? Is there any chance that I'm going to get super strength in my hand? Because I'm not gonna lie, that would be stupendous..."

What does that sample tell you about the character?

It tells me that Flynn's someone who likes expensive things and will do anything to get them. Even steal. He thinks a lot about himself and what he can get from people or out of a situation.

Does this character have a catch phrase? What is it?

He doesn't have a catch phrase, but everything he says is like a joke. He's pretty confident about himself too.

How does this character react to other characters?

To the other thieves he betrayed – He tries to avoid them. To Rapunzel – He tries to figure her out.

If you were to have a phone conversation with this character, what would it sound like?

Me: Hey, Flynn. Flynn: Hey. You want to be part of my fan club, don't you? Well, the group is large, but I suppose we have room for one more.

Activity #4.3

VOICE THAT REVEALS CHARACTER

Students are exposed to good examples of character voice and experiment with their own fictional characters' voices.

NEED

- **Voice that Reveals Character** graphic organizers (one per student)
- **Character Traits** sheet (page 20)
- appropriate level books/excerpts with well-developed character voices
- Writer's Notebooks

TIME: 45 MINUTES

- 15 minutes to share published examples of voice
- 15 minutes to complete **Voice that Reveals Character** graphic organizer and write scene
- 15 minutes for follow-up sharing and discussion

SUGGESTED TEXTS

Clementine by Sarah Pennypacker (see Suggested Texts chart, pages 99-100, for more)

COMMON CORE ANCHOR STANDARDS

WRITING:

W.3 Write narratives to develop real or imagined experiences or events using effective technique, well-chosen details and well-structured event sequences.

LANGUAGE:

L.3 Apply knowledge of language to understand how language functions in different contexts, to make effective choices for meaning or style, and to comprehend more fully when reading or listening.

READING:

RL.3 Describe in depth a character, setting, or event in a story or drama, drawing on specific details in the text (e.g., a character's thoughts, words, or actions).

WHAT TO DO

1 Share examples of published work, such as Sarah Pennypacker's *Clementine*, that use voice to reveal character. Have students identify the character trait the author is trying to illustrate in the excerpt. The **Character Traits** sheet (page 20) may be helpful. If using *Clementine*, select an excerpt that has an "Okay, fine," in it. This catch phrase lets readers know, loud and clear, that it's Clementine's voice. It is used throughout the book and readers learn to expect her to say it.

2. Students write a short scene in their Writer's Notebooks in which they reveal a certain character trait. Have students use the **Voice that Reveals Character** choice sheet to set up their writing piece, unless they are immediately able to write using their own fictional characters.
3. Pair students to have them share their scenes.
4. Choose a few students to read their scenes to the whole class. Ask listeners to identify the character trait being revealed in the shared samples.

ASSESSMENT

Completed scenes can be collected and evaluated as assessment pieces.

Name: ______________________ Date: ______________

Voice that Reveals Character

DIRECTIONS

Select one of the seven choices of character and scene. Answer the Questions to Think About. Then write for fifteen minutes in your Writer's Notebook. Try to reveal character traits through things the character says, thinks, and does. Think carefully about your word choice.

	CHARACTER	SCENE	CHARACTER TRAIT
1	a young boy	playing baseball	determined
2	a dog	sitting in his doghouse	lonely
3	twins	arguing over a toy	stubborn
4	a mother	getting a present	grateful
5	an orange	being packed into a lunchbox	afraid
6	a pencil	being sharpened	confused
7	a dancer	putting on a show	excited

QUESTIONS TO THINK ABOUT

What will the character do?______________________

____

____

What will the character think? ______________________

____

____

What will the character say?______________________

____

____

How can you show, not tell the reader what character trait you are revealing?

____

____

Name: ______________________ Date: __________

Voice that Reveals Character

DIRECTIONS

Select one of the seven choices of character and scene. Answer the Questions to Think About. Then write for fifteen minutes in your Writer's Notebook. Try to reveal character traits through things the character says, thinks, and does. Think carefully about your word choice.

	CHARACTER	SCENE	CHARACTER TRAIT
1	a young boy	playing baseball	determined
2	a dog	sitting in his doghouse	lonely
3	twins	arguing over a toy	stubborn
4	a mother	getting a present	grateful
5	an orange	being packed into a lunchbox	afraid
6	a pencil	being sharpened	confused
7	a dancer	putting on a show	excited

QUESTIONS TO THINK ABOUT

What will the character do? Orange will talk to Sandwich

What will the character think? Orange will be excited to be going in the lunchbox, finally!

What will the character say? Orange will tell Sandwich how happy he is, until Sand wich tells Orange it's not good to go in the lunchbox

How can you show, not tell the reader what character trait you are revealing?
Orange will be happy. Then start screeching. Then get quiet.

VOICE THAT REVEALS CHARACTER

Sample Entry in Writer's Notebook

Voice that Reveals Character – #5: an orange being packed into a lunchbox, afraid

"Oh, that was a great scrub under the faucet. Look at me! My peel is all clean and shiny. I have an awesome feeling about today, don't you, Sandwich?" Orange admired herself in the metal surface of the toaster.

"If by awesome, you mean horrible, then yes. I have the same feeling." Sandwich blew out a breath of bread crumbs.

"Horrible? Why would you feel—" Orange's words got cut off as Heather grabbed her and tossed her into a cold, hard box.

"Where am I? Sandwich! Sandwich! What's going on?" Her voice was screechy. Drops of orange juice beaded up on her peel as Heather closed a massive flap and all the light disappeared.

A loud zzzipppp-zzzipp sounded around the edges of the box, and it was just Orange and the cold blackness inside the box. She shivered.

"Get me out of here!"

"Calm down," a voice said behind her.

"Sandwich?"

"Yeah, do you still feel awesome about today? It's our turn."

"Our turn for what?"

"Lunch."

Activity #4.4

WHICH POINT OF VIEW?

Students choose the point of view that will work best for their characters and the story they wish to tell.

NEED

- Writer's Notebooks

TIME: 45 MINUTES

- 30 minutes to write scenes
- 15 minutes follow-up sharing and discussion

COMMON CORE ANCHOR STANDARDS

WRITING:

W.3 Write narratives to develop real or imagined experiences or events using effective technique, well-chosen details and well-structured event sequences.

LANGUAGE:

L.3 Apply knowledge of language to understand how language functions in different contexts, to make effective choices for meaning or style, and to comprehend more fully when reading or listening.

READING:

RL.6 Assess how point of view or purpose shapes the content and style of a text.

WHAT TO DO

1. Start with a full discussion of the concept of Point of View. The information on pages 77-79 might be helpful for guiding your discussion.
2. In their Writer's Notebooks, students write part of their characters' stories in first person, then another part in third person.
3. When they have finished writing, students should re-read both versions.
4. Students share with some trusted critique buddies in the classroom. Have students use each other as a sounding board for what point of view is most effective. Students should ask each other which version grabs their attention and holds their interest better. Students should feel free to ask the teacher's opinion, too (although they usually don't need it once they've talked to their writing peers).

Activity #4.5

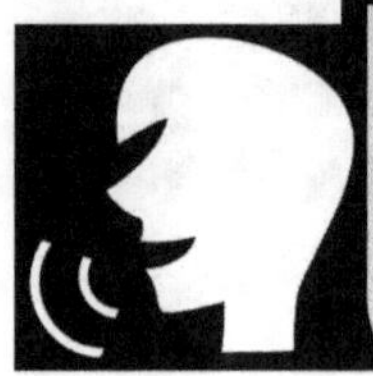

DIFFERENT HATS

NEED

- **Different Hats** scenarios (one per student)
- Writer's Notebooks

TIME: 45 MINUTES

- 30 minutes to write scenes
- 15 minutes follow-up sharing and discussion

COMMON CORE ANCHOR STANDARDS

WRITING:
W.3 Write narratives to develop real or imagined experiences or events using effective technique, well-chosen details and well-structured event sequences.

LANGUAGE:
L.3 Apply knowledge of language to understand how language functions in different contexts, to make effective choices for meaning or style, and to comprehend more fully when reading or listening.

READING:
RL.6 Assess how point of view or purpose shapes the content and style of a text.

WHAT TO DO

1. Students read the seven **Different Hats** scenarios and perspective choices.
2. Students choose one scenario. In their Writer's Notebooks, they write the same scene from two different perspectives. Point of view can be either first or third person. Students must think of how two different characters would react to the scene. Students should capture what is different about the two perspectives and create two distinct voices.
3. Students share their scenes aloud with the class, without saying which perspective they are reading. The rest of the class should be able to tell based on the content.

ASSESSMENT

Use the **Checklist for Different Hats** to assess this exercise.

Name: ______________________________ Date: ____________

Different Hats

DIRECTIONS

Select one of the seven scenarios below. Write about it using the two different perspectives provided. It should be the same scene, but with characters who view the scene very differently. As always, use word choice that *shows* what is happening rather than *tells*.

1 A surprise birthday party from the perspective of:
   - A a ten-year old
   - B an older person who dislikes birthdays

2 Eating a big bowl of ice cream with hot fudge from the perspective of:
   - A someone who has spent the day working outside in the hot summer sunshine
   - B someone who is supposed to be on a diet to get in shape

3 A championship soccer game from the perspective of:
   - A a player on the winning team
   - B a player on the losing team

4 A snowstorm from the perspective of:
   - A a student who just heard school is cancelled
   - B a traveler whose flight home just got cancelled

5 The first day of school from the perspective of:
   - A a new student
   - B a class pet (hamster, lizard, fish, bird, hermit crab, etc.)

6 Winning a prize from the perspective of:
   - A an outgoing, confident person
   - B a shy, quiet person

7 Getting a puppy from the perspective of:
   - A someone who always wanted a dog
   - B someone who is allergic to dogs

DIFFERENT HATS

Sample Entry in Writer's Notebook

Different Hats – A snowstorm from the perspective of:

* a student who just heard school is cancelled
* a traveler whose flight home just got cancelled

Student: Yippeeee! I jumped out of bed as soon as Mom came in to say that school was cancelled because of the snowstorm. I raced through breakfast, spent ten minutes bundling up into my snowsuit and boots, and burst through the back door into the yard.

Everything was covered in white. No one had made any tracks yet. They had left that up to me, and I wasn't going to let anyone down. Bounding down the patio stairs, I hopped, galloped, shuffled, twirled, and ran through the snow, leaving crazy designs behind me.

I built a snow dog and named him Flakes. We played catch with a snowball, but Flakes just refused to run. Lazy snow dog. I had more luck with my snow fort, which protected me from Crazy Callie next door. She kept throwing shovelfuls of snow at me until her mother called her inside.

Then my own mother called me inside with a mug of hot chocolate in her hand. I couldn't resist. I peeled off my snowsuit and sipped the hot chocolate on the couch while watching my favorite shows.

What a great snow day!

Traveler: Cancelled! No, no, no. My flight cannot be cancelled. I squeezed my eyes shut then looked up at the board again. The word cancelled was still there next to my flight number.

All around me, passengers in the airport scurried around trying to make other plans to get out of New York. From the sounds of things, I didn't think they were having any luck. No one was. Not today.

Today we were stuck like flies on peanut butter.

Did I mention I was allergic to peanut butter?

Sigh.

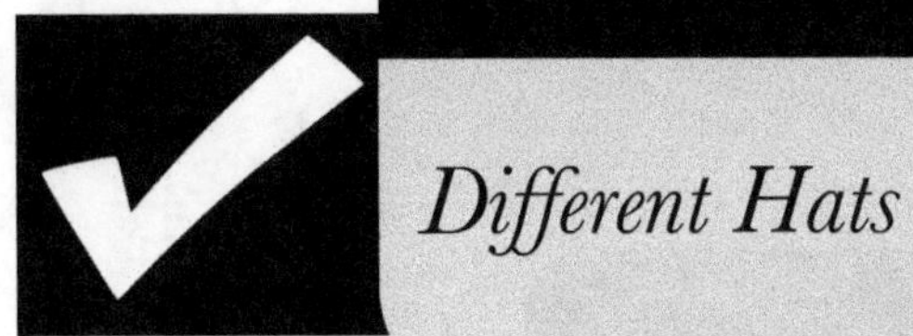

Different Hats

DIFFERENT HATS	DIFFERENT HATS
Student Name: ______ Date: ______ ☐ Scene is well described using sensory details and vivid word choice. ☐ Perspectives are unique and clearly developed. ☐ Different voices are present and interesting to read. Comments: ______	Student Name: ______ Date: ______ ☐ Scene is well described using sensory details and vivid word choice. ☐ Perspectives are unique and clearly developed. ☐ Different voices are present and interesting to read. Comments: ______
DIFFERENT HATS	**DIFFERENT HATS**
Student Name: ______ Date: ______ ☐ Scene is well described using sensory details and vivid word choice. ☐ Perspectives are unique and clearly developed. ☐ Different voices are present and interesting to read. Comments: ______	Student Name: ______ Date: ______ ☐ Scene is well described using sensory details and vivid word choice. ☐ Perspectives are unique and clearly developed. ☐ Different voices are present and interesting to read. Comments: ______
DIFFERENT HATS	**DIFFERENT HATS**
Student Name: ______ Date: ______ ☐ Scene is well described using sensory details and vivid word choice. ☐ Perspectives are unique and clearly developed. ☐ Different voices are present and interesting to read. Comments: ______	Student Name: ______ Date: ______ ☐ Scene is well described using sensory details and vivid word choice. ☐ Perspectives are unique and clearly developed. ☐ Different voices are present and interesting to read. Comments: ______

NEXT STEPS

Students have now spent a great deal of time thinking about characters in general and their own specific characters. They have studied existing characters from published authors to uncover what works. They have also experimented with the many layers of their own characters. This deep understanding of what makes a believable, realistic character is necessary before students enter the world of setting and plot development. Only when the characters' voices are loud, demanding to have their stories written, will students be ready to write. The work done before the actual writing is critical to creating characters that leap off the page and grab readers' attention.

Through observation, interviewing, planning for change, and playing with voice, dialogue, and point of view, students have done the work of real authors. The results are characters who have a three-dimensional feel, are dynamic, and are ready to face the obstacles that stand in their way.

At this point, the characters students have been developing should be ready to burst free. Time to unleash! Assign the task of actually writing the stories these characters have been preparing to star in. Students have thought about events in the **Character Change** activity and setting in the **Habitat** activity, but you may need to do some additional work on the story elements of setting and plot for students to have all the pieces they need to create stories that will entertain readers.

Happy writing!

Appendix A: Suggested Texts

SUGGESTED TEXTS BY GRADE LEVEL

Any work of fiction (both picture and chapter books) can be used for the lessons and activities outlined in this book, as long as there is a strong character that illustrates the concepts and features of good characterization. This chart gives you a place to start in your book collection, but I encourage you to read many different books and always be on the hunt for fabulous characters. You don't need to use a book in its entirety. Reading a character-focused snippet is often enough to show students how the author has crafted a character that will stick with readers. While age-appropriateness is always a concern, look for opportunities to share complex characters even if you might not recommend the entire story to your students.

GRADE 3	
Title	**Author**
Ramona Quimby, Age 8	Beverly Cleary
Gooney Bird Greene	Lois Lowry
Clementine	Sarah Pennypacker
Albert	Donna Jo Napoli
Fireflies	Judy Brinckloe
Verdi and *Stellaluna*	Janell Cannon
Charlotte's Web	E. B. White

GRADE 4	
Title	**Author**
The Paper Bag Princess	Robert Munsch
The Lemonade War	Jacqueline Davies
Old Jake's Skirts	Anne C. Scott
Harry Potter and the Sorcerer's Stone	J. K. Rowling
The City of Ember	Jeanne DuPrau
Because of Winn Dixie	Kate DiCamillo
Frindle	Andrew Clements

GRADE 5	
Title	**Author**
Thank You, Mr. Falker	Patricia Polacco
Walk Two Moons	Sharon Creech
Pictures of Hollis Woods	Patricia Reilly Giff
Love, Aubrey	Suzanne LaFleur
The Giver	Lois Lowry
The Lightning Thief	Rick Riordan
The Sign of the Beaver	Elizabeth George Speare

GRADES 6-8	
Title	**Author**
Anne of Green Gables	Lucy Maud Montgomery
The Hunger Games	Suzanne Collins
Stormbreaker	Anthony Horowitz
Smile (graphic novel)	Raina Telgemeier
The Lion, the Witch and the Wardrobe	C. S. Lewis
Crispin: The Cross of Lead	Avi
Hoot	Carl Hiaasen

Appendix A: Suggested Texts

BIBLIOGRAPHY

Avi, *Crispin: The Cross of Lead*. New York: Hyperion Books, 2004.

Brinckloe, Julie. *Fireflies.* New York: Aladdin, 1986.

Cannon, Janell. *Verdi.* New York: Harcourt Children's Books, 1997.

Cannon, Janell. *Stellaluna.* Boston: HMH Books, 2007.

Cleary, Beverly. *Ramona Quimby, Age 8.* New York: HarperCollins, 2009.

Clements, Andrew. *Frindle.* New York: Atheneum Books for Young Readers, 1998.

Collins, Suzanne. *The Hunger Games.* New York: Scholastic, 2009.

Creech, Sharon. *Walk Two Moons.* New York: HarperCollins, 2009.

Davies, Jacqueline. *The Lemonade War.* Boston: Houghton Mifflin Books for Children, 2009.

DiCamillo, Kate. *Because of Winn-Dixie.* Somerville: Candlewick Press, 2009.

DuPrau, Jeanne. *The City of Ember.* New York: Random House Books for Young Readers, 2003.

Giff, Patricia Reilly. *Pictures of Hollis Woods.* New York: Yearling Books, 2008.

Green, John. *Looking for Alaska.* New York: Speak, 2008.

Hiaasen, Carl. *Hoot.* New York: Yearling Books, 2005.

Horowitz, Anthony. *Stormbreaker.* London: Puffin, 2006.

LaFleur, Suzanne. *Love, Aubrey.* New York: Wendy Lamb Books, 2009.

Lewis, C. S. *The Lion, the Witch and the Wardrobe.* New York: HarperCollins, 1994.

Lowry, Lois. *Gooney Bird Greene.* Boston: Houghton Mifflin Books for Children, 2010.

Lowry, Lois. *The Giver.* New York: Laurel Leaf, 2002.

Montgomery, Lucy Maud. *Anne of Green Gables*. New York: Laurel Leaf, 1997.

Munsch, Robert. *The Paper Bag Princess.* Toronto: Annick Press, 1992.

Napoli, Donna Jo. *Albert.* New York: Sandpiper, 2005.

Pennypacker, Sara. *Clementine.* New York: Hyperion Books, 2008.

Polacco, Patricia. *Thank You, Mr. Falker.* New York: Philomel, 1998.

Riordan, Rick. *The Lightning Thief.* New York: Disney Hyperion, 2009.

Rowling, J. K. *Harry Potter and the Sorcerer's Stone.* New York: Scholastic, 1999.

Telgemeier, Raina. *Smile*. New York: Graphix, 2010.

Scott, Anne C. *Old Jake's Skirts.* Lanham: Cooper Square Publishing, 2003.

Speare, Elizabeth George. *The Sign of the Beaver.* New York: Houghton Mifflin, 1983.

White, E. B. *Charlotte's Web.* New York: HarperCollins, 2006.

Appendix B: Student Resources

GLOSSARY

character – a person (sometimes an animal, inanimate object, or creature) in a story

character change – the growth a character shows from the beginning of a story to the end

character trait – describes features of a character's personality (friendly, aggressive, humorous)

conflict – the problem, obstacle, or struggle that a character faces in a story

dialogue – conversation between characters in a story

eavesdrop – to listen to conversation

fiction – a made-up story

flaw – a weakness

goal – something a character wants

habitat – the place where a character spends his/her/its time

interview – to ask questions in order to learn more about someone

motivation – what causes a character to want to reach a goal

narrative – a story

narrator – the person who is telling the story

observe – to look at closely

physical appearance – what a character looks like (for example, hair color, eye color, body type, facial features, clothing, scars)

point of view – the perspective from which a story is told. First person point of view uses *I*, *me*, and *my*. Third person point of view uses *he*, *she*, *they*, and the characters' names.

show, don't tell – refers to describing the character through actions, thoughts, and dialogue rather than merely telling the readers about the character

voice – the style of writing that makes the author's writing unique. Voice also refers to a character's style of narrating the story.

WRITER'S WORD CARDS

Display these words in the writing classroom for students to refer to while thinking and writing in the Writing Workshop. You can make copies of this page for students to keep in their Writer's Notebooks. Encourage students to use these terms when discussing their writing.

character	character change
character trait	conflict
dialogue	flaw
goal	interview
motivation	narrative
narrator	observe
physical appearance	point of view
show, don't tell	voice

character	character change
character trait	conflict

flaw	interview
dialogue	goal

narrative	observe
motivation	narrator

physical appearance	voice
point of view	show, don't tell

PROFESSIONAL BOOKS

Browne, Renni and Dave King. *Self-Editing for Fiction Writers.* New York: HarperCollins, 2004.

Burroway, Janet, Elizabeth Stuckey-French, and Ned Stuckey-French. *Writing Fiction: A Guide to Narrative Craft.* White Plains: Pearson Longman, 2010.

Culham, Ruth. *6 + 1 Traits of Writing: The Complete Guide, Grades 3 and Up.* New York: Scholastic, Inc., 2003.

Fletcher, Ralph and JoAnn Portalupi. *Writing Workshop: The Essential Guide.* Portsmouth: Heinemann, 2001.

Heard, Georgia. *The Revision Toolbox: Teaching Techniques that Work.* Portsmouth: Heinemann, 2003.

Levine, Gail Carson. *Writing Magic: Creating Stories that Fly.* New York: HarperCollins, 2006.

Murray, Donald. *A Writer Teaches Writing.* Independence: Wadsworth Publishing, 2003.

Ray, Katie Wood. *The Writer's Workshop: Working through the Hard Parts (And They're All Hard Parts).* Urbana: National Council of Teachers of English, 2001.

Strunk, William and E. B. White. *The Elements of Style.* New York: Longman Publishers, 2000.

WEBSITES

COMMON CORE STATE STANDARDS:
www.corestandards.org

ALWAYS WRITE:
corbettharrison.com

RALPH FLETCHER:
www.ralphfletcher.com

READWRITETHINK:
www.readwritethink.org

NATIONAL COUNCIL OF TEACHERS OF ENGLISH:
www.ncte.org

WRITINGFIX:
www.writingfix.com

TEACHERS & WRITERS COLLABORATIVE:
www.twc.org

SOCIETY OF CHILDREN'S BOOK WRITERS AND ILLUSTRATORS:
www.scbwi.org

ABOUT THE AUTHOR

Christine DePetrillo is a teacher and author. She has been an elementary educator since 1997 and holds a Master's degree in elementary education from Rhode Island College. She believes strongly in giving students experiences that will set them up for success in the real world. For her, the classroom is not a separate place from society, but a vital component in keeping that society going for generations to come.

Christine is the author of many works of fiction, all of which end with a "happily ever after." She is multi-published in a variety of genres including contemporary romance, paranormal romance, romantic suspense, historical romance, young adult romance (writing as Christy Major), and gothic poetry.

ABOUT COMPASS PUBLISHING

Compass Publishing is the educational book imprint of Brigantine Media. Materials that are created by experienced education practitioners are the hallmark of Compass Publishing resources. For more information, please contact:

Neil Raphel
Brigantine Media | 211 North Avenue | St. Johnsbury, Vermont | 05819

Phone: 802-751-8802
E-mail: neil@brigantinemedia.com | Website: www.brigantinemedia.com